It shouldn't happen to a
TEACHER

by
David Franklin

with

Bretwalda Books
Unit 8, Fir Tree Close, Epsom,
Surrey KT17 3LD

info@BretwaldaBooks.com
www.BretwaldaBooks.com

ISBN 978-1-909099-15-9

Bretwalda Books Ltd

CONTENTS

FOREWORD

It was, I suppose, no great surprise when the author announced that he had written a book based on his experiences as schoolteacher, deputy headmaster, and youth leader. I have known him for some 40 years and heard some of these incidents before. His life has been packed full of activity and incidents; and to describe him as dynamic is a bit like remarking that Ian Botham was a decent cricketer. He also has the ability to tell, and write, a good story, as you, I hope, are about to find out.

The book has that happy mix of being entertaining - sometimes very funny – and yet leaving the reader with some serious points to consider. I certainly found the book very difficult to put down once I had started reading, and was thoroughly entertained. Many of us will be absorbed by the accounts of how things used to be done, the strong but consistent discipline, the "short, sharp shock", and the sensible ways of tackling conflicts and awkward situations. Have things improved?

The author has been passionate throughout his life about helping young people, mentally, physically, and spiritually. In this age of political correctness, some of it unbelievably daft, he is blessed with common sense, as well as strong leadership skills, and, I am pleased to say, a huge sense of fun.

And that is my last point. This book is fun. I hope that, like me, you enjoy it.

Stuart Barnes

INTRODUCTION

As far as I can remember, my primary school had no written rules. Everyone knew the difference between right and wrong and if anyone transgressed – male or female – they got smacked. Everyone understood, no child objected, no parents complained. It was not child abuse (a phrase yet to be invented) and was called "discipline". Simple!

I don't think my grammar school had any written rules either but I do remember the deputy head standing up in assembly one morning and booming: "Some of you are not sure about the school rules. We only have one: DO AS YOU'RE TOLD!" Regrettably for me, I didn't do as I was told from day one which resulted in several painful interviews with him. Too late did the penny drop, by which time I had no chance of going to Oxbridge because I had fooled about in Latin; no chance of becoming an engineer because I had fooled about in Physics; and no chance of becoming a linguist because I had fooled about in French. Later, as a prefect and then school captain, I became a poacher turned gamekeeper and bitterly regret my misspent youth which cost me dear and was the main reason I always did my very best to direct straying pupils back on to the straight and narrow by whatever means I felt most appropriate at the time.

Throughout my teaching profession I witnessed many unbelievable incidents and one day vowed to write a book based on my scribbled notes. However, always being extremely busy with teaching, sport, youth work, church, family etc., I never got round to it. I did pen a few articles for *Parentwise* magazine in 1993 but there were never enough hours in the day to do justice to an extremely varied career working with children.

I taught in every type of school, all social classes and ages ranging from 8-18, so I am well qualified to comment on the disasters which overtook the education system in the later stages of the 20th Century. The rot began during the liberal 1960s and when corporal punishment was abolished in the mid-1980s the lunatics were well and truly in charge of the working class asylums. Middle class parents voted with their feet and very soon what I had always predicted came about – with comprehensive schools becoming socially and academically divided into middle and working class ghettos – with politicians and so-called educationists blaming failing results on increasingly hard-pressed and over-worked teachers. Stuff and nonsense! As I will show, it was perfectly possible to make a silk purse out of a sow's ear but only if the sow and her piglets were strictly controlled by the farmer. Anything less was a recipe for failure which we now see all around us, especially for the underclass, the brightest of whom once had a way out through the grammar school system.

I have no time for those who pontificate and rarely get their hands dirty but all the time in the world for the humble classroom practitioner who gets on with the job both inside and outside school. Turn over and chuckle/gasp/cry at what you read. It's all true – well 95% of it anyway! Every single story, however, is based on a true incident which took place sometime during the last 50 years.

****

CARTOONS

The brilliant cartoons are by Ken Wilkins who once drew *Dennis the Menace* in *The Beano*. My grateful thanks to him for all his ongoing support while the book was being written.

****

DEDICATION

I dedicate this book to the thousands of pupils and parents who enriched my life over six decades. Many others, though, caused me great anguish as any teacher reading this paragraph will readily understand. I was sworn at, threatened and even attacked outside my own home by a drug addict who blamed me for his problems. Overall, however, the good outweighed the bad and I count it a privilege to remain in touch with a large number, some of whom are now close to retirement themselves.

David Franklin

February 2012

CHILDHOOD

Childhood is a relatively recent phenomenon, less than two centuries old. Until the great Victorian philanthropists and reformers came along – virtually every one of them a practising Christian – the word "children" simply meant "offspring" and an extension of the family who went to work at the earliest possible opportunity. For the vast majority of people there was no privacy of any kind and survival was the name of the game. Things we now take for granted, such as free schooling and medical care, pensions, state benefit, or simply learning to swim in a public pool, simply did not exist.

It is a far cry from today when, paradoxically, child protection laws have done virtually the opposite of what had been intended. The element of risk and self discovery for children has almost disappeared and although self-styled experts will point to improved statistics they are not at all comparable when

one realises children in the past were allowed to roam free far from their homes, without any form of adult supervision. Nowadays they are often wrapped up in cotton wool, especially where school activities are concerned, because of the very real fear of litigation should an accident occur. Many of retirement age cannot understand how such a situation was ever allowed to evolve and think it blindingly obvious that increasingly poor behaviour is closely linked to the disappearance of childhood and the spread of pornography. How on earth did we allow the phrase "bad behaviour" to evolve into "challenging behaviour" and why are we surprised that a daily diet of TV and online screen violence perpetuates aggression and selfishness?

Neil Postman, an American academic, wrote several books, two of which are particularly pertinent to this volume. *The Disappearance of Childhood* (1982) explains how, when, where and why we lost the plot and both betrayed and destroyed our offspring when they should have been growing up and innocently discovering the world around them. *Amusing Ourselves to Death* (1985) goes one stage further and shows how the western world has degenerated into an obsession with celebrities and money, the results of which are only too plain to see. In 1990 he gave a lecture entitled *Informing Ourselves to Death* in which he argued the Western world is drowning in information over which it no longer has control, and doesn't know how to cope with it.

The following pages belong to a gentler age when teachers were respected by both pupils and parents alike, and when learning was seen to be beneficial for the whole community. It is in this context that you are invited to turn back the clock and see what it was like before the monster called "Political Correctness" reared its ugly head. Forget the present – enjoy the past.

TROUBLE ON THE COACH

Teaching was in the family blood with all my mother's three siblings and one of father's, all involved at various levels. Catastrophe overtook us all, however, when my mother died of cancer aged just 42, leaving behind a ruined linear and extended family too painful to describe in print. I loved school, though, and never seriously considered any other career so decided to see what experience I could get while still in the sixth form. Teaching first formers in my own school whilst school captain was easy but another venture just a few miles away opened my eyes to reality.

When I approached the local education authority to ask if I could spend my half term teaching in one of their schools they were more than happy and allocated me to a secondary modern which I passed every day on my way to school on the train. I enjoyed it and learnt a lot. Let me explain .....

The first thing I noticed was their extremely broad Lancashire accents. I had an accent too, although was not really aware of it, but these children were different. They lived mainly in terraced houses with communal toilets at the end of the street or, if they were lucky, down the end of their own backyard. I did not realise this at the time however, only a couple of years later when carrying out a town planning survey vacation job to make ends meet at university.

Back to "The Ranch" which I mean literally. For one whole morning I was placed in charge of a group of 14/15 year olds who had very few brain cells and were therefore not bright enough to cause any serious trouble. They were also separated from the main school and operated from an annexe amusingly referred to as "The Ranch", this at a time when cowboy dramas had just started to appear on black and white television with the phrase "Meanwhile, back at the ranch ..." seemingly part of the dialogue in every one of them.

Being a keen geographer and geologist I thought I would amuse these urchins by talking about hills, rocks, landscape features etc. My first question about different types of rocks, though, brought totally blank expressions so I tried again. "Look out of the window and tell me what that range of hills is called." Nothing. "Well what are they made of?" Still nothing. "Who can tell me the name of a rock?" Looks of utter bewilderment but still the penny hadn't dropped – my penny, not theirs. "Who's ever seen a rock?"

"Me sir!" screeched the smallest and most pathetic specimen which brought an instant response from a much larger specimen: "Please sir, he's a liar. He's never been out of

Radcliffe in his life!" The penny suddenly fell noisily to the floor. These children had never been anywhere, not even outside their own little town, and had no idea what a rock was nor the name of the Pennine Hills which were clearly visible in the distance every day of their lives. Actually … one boy had been elsewhere because he had just arrived from Shropshire and was therefore better qualified to answer my next question. "Who knows where Manchester is?" Silence apart from the new Salopian who said "Please sir, is it in England?" By now I was beginning to appreciate their narrow horizons. Manchester was four miles away at one end of the railway line which clearly none of them had ever travelled on, and yet which I used six days a week.

I tried again. "Does anyone know where Bury is?" Bury was the next town, just a few hundred yards down the main road and the terminus of the aforesaid railway line. Not only did they not know – they had never heard of it! I rest my case but they all probably ended up perfectly happily in a manual job earning enough money to keep them and their families ticking over.

****

As a postscript, shortly before moving on to Cambridge for my post-graduate teaching certificate, I also spent a week in another secondary modern which, although perhaps a couple of miles from Radcliffe was a world apart. The children were still largely working class but this was a church school in new buildings where uniform was smart, and standards were high because they could pick and choose whom they accepted. I really enjoyed my time there but was taken aback when a 13 year old girl knocked on the staff room door one lunchtime and said "Please sir, can you come and turn the showers on for us?" I politely declined and asked the senior mistress if she would oblige. How childhood has changed!

Teaching there was a pleasure which is not surprising when one considers that a whole class, some of whose members had cheeked a teacher, were ordered to stay in silence for a whole week. Imagine it – a class today actually remaining silent for a whole week – but they did – and they learnt their lesson. Wow!

You will not be surprised to discover this school later became a high achieving comprehensive which soon outstripped the former state grammar school down the road.

****

Out of sequence but for the sake of convenience, I now include a few observations on a couple of weeks I spent teaching English as a foreign language at a large institution in Cambridge for whom I had previously worked as a warden at one of their hostels earlier in the year. Their clients were extremely wealthy and from all over Europe, mostly pleasant but some extremely arrogant with egos to match. Happily, the senior managers had their measure.

When I refereed a kick-about football match and awarded a goal for some random team I was amazed to be shouted at by two Spanish teenagers who said, I quote "You English, you cheat all the time, just like the World Cup!" I could not believe my ears but then I was still relatively young. Sadly, they honestly believed England had cheated in winning the World Cup the previous year.

I must have seemed the part, however, because I was placed in control of four other university graduates to lead two coach loads of foreign students for a day out to Great Yarmouth, some of whom were not much younger than us. Before we began I was handed enough cash to buy lunch for 100 at any hotel I could find and then barter with them. True – and it worked but an incident occurred on the way at which I still shudder, although at the time it seemed the natural thing to do!

The back seat on my coach was quickly commandeered by some noisy Italian boys who liked to show off to the girls. I warned them before we started that they must be sensible or there would be trouble but they clearly thought I was bluffing because once underway they started to cause a nuisance. The driver, quite rightly, objected so I told him to pick out the culprits in his rear view mirror and I would take action. I did! First, they were warned they would be put off the coach if they persisted, at which they calmed down – but not for long. After no more than another few minutes down the road the driver quietly informed me they were still messing about so I again asked him to identify the culprits, which he did – two boys aged about 14. I then ordered him to stop the coach just as we were passing Newmarket racecourse.

Silence ensued as I marched to the back, picked out the two ringleaders and, pointing to the door at the front said, very loudly: "Out!" You could have heard the proverbial pin drop. Like little lambs they meekly climbed off whereupon I loudly told them to find their own way back to Cambridge. I knew they had enough money but even so, just imagine what would have happened in today's politically correct climate. The press would have had a field day but I doubt the boys ever told their parents. Authority was still largely respected back in 1967 and the boys eventually hitch-hiked their way back home.

A relieving sense of order and calm descended as we left them standing by the roadside followed by a great day on the East Anglian coast where I was amused to discover the French students did not expect to change on the beach for a dip in the sea. "Les Frogs" were obviously more prudish than the leaders had been led to believe. On return to Cambridge I expected a mild reprimand but was congratulated on my actions and the troublemakers behaved themselves for the rest of the week! I rest my case, m'lud!

★★★★★★★★★★★★★★★★★★★★★★★★

Again out of sequence but just to prove lightning can sometimes strike twice, during my second year of teaching I left a further young person behind after he deliberately disobeyed instructions to get back on the coach. In charge of the weekly first form swimming trip to a town a few miles away I ran everything like clockwork and always ensured nobody was late at either end of the expedition. The children got the very best from their swim and several passed various examinations but there was never any time for messing about if we were to return on time.

One new boy rivalled Billy Bunter in appearance and it was not hard to see why. Unlike his smaller older brother who was eminently sensible and obedient, William George Bunter was fond of his food, too fond as he quickly found out one day, as he was polishing off another bag of crisps and playing the machines in the swimming pool foyer. As he was delaying our departure I ordered him back on the coach, only to be ignored. "Get back on the coach – now!" brought a grunt so I gave him a final ultimatum "Get on the coach – now – or we will leave you behind!" Still he didn't believe me so I told the driver to start the engine and depart.

The Fat Owl of the Remove suddenly got the message and, abandoning his one-armed bandit but still clutching his swimming gear and half-eaten bag of crisps, waddled as fast as he could to cut us off at the exit to the car park. The driver slowed down, looked at me and said "Shall I let him on, sir?" "No!" was my thundering reply and off we went leaving William G. stranded. I duly reported what had happened to the school office on my return, at which point the gallant caretaker set off to collect him. Far from being given a dressing down, however, the headmaster praised my actions and the Fat Owl left the school a few weeks later when it became increasingly obvious he was totally unsuited to the academic rigour and required standards of behaviour.

Things were different in those days!

TEACHING PRACTICE

My post-graduate year was spent at Cambridge University where I enjoyed spells in both my college football and tennis teams. For the term in between I stayed at the Cambridge University Mission in Bermondsey, in the heart of what was then London's dockland area on the south bank of the River Thames. I commuted daily to a Direct Grant School where I enjoyed a most interesting and informative few weeks. During the day I mixed with largely middle class children but in the evenings I helped with deprived children of a very different kind.

Bermondsey's most famous son, singer Tommy Steele, was typical of the none too bright lads I dealt with at the CUM. If

they took a shine to you then that was fine but if they didn't you were in for a difficult time. Age did not matter and when I first took a group of primary school age boys down into the rifle range one of them immediately shot another one in the foot. It was a salutary lesson that children often disobey the most obvious and simple rules, and stood me in good stead for a few years down the line when I became deputy headmaster of a working class inner urban school 150 miles away in a provincial county town.

A number of incidents spring to mind from my teaching practice:

The eldest of three sons of a famous pop singer drove his father's Rolls Royce to school every day while the head of P.E. arrived on his bike. Sadly, the still young pop singer dropped dead from a heart attack just after I left.

While teaching a group of 13-year-olds, the form captain announced how all clever boys lived in the suburbs while those less bright lived in the inner city. Sitting next to him was the vice captain who travelled on the same train as me from Bermondsey and who looked me straight in the eye as much as to say "That's all he knows!" I gave him a wink to let him know I understood but did not give the game away because the two were close friends.

I unwittingly pulled out a clump of hair from a boy's head when I responded to his pleasantly cheeky manner by twisting his whiskers only to see them part company from their roots as he instinctively backed away. My quick response was "You're moulting" but deep down I was stunned. All he could say was "It's not funny, sir!" Indeed it wasn't.

A first year boy who also lived in the Docklands area begged to be allowed to accompany me home on the train which I caught immediately after school on the days when I was not involved in extra-curricular activities. When I asked why he explained how his school was banned from being on the station at the same time as the local boys comprehensive school. Further investigations revealed one of our boys had actually been thrown on to the electric line in a previous fracas. The other school was later closed down, renamed and reopened with a new identity.

All boys in the first and second forms (Years 7 and 8) had to wear short trousers. This was no big deal at the time but it was for a boy who lived near the Old Kent Road. To avoid trouble he wore long trousers over the top of his shorts until he reached Peckham Rye when all the local comprehensive school boys got off. Only in this way could he avoid ridicule.

★★★★★★★★★★★★★★★★★★★★★★★

I learnt a great deal in a very short space of time and will be forever grateful for the opportunities I was afforded.

THE BARE TRUTH

It is hard to believe what went on in education 40-50 years ago. The modern educational theorist would say things have improved and in many ways they have. In other respects, however, there has been a marked decline in morals, discipline, educational standards (although not in knowledge), the family unit and general respect for others – especially for older people. In terms of the real bare truth I found it both depressing and unbelievable that my grandson, in his first year at comprehensive school, never got his knees dirty in games and never went anywhere near a communal shower – nor an individual one. How did we win the Battle of Waterloo? How times have changed!

I didn't know it but when I began teaching in a boys grammar school the pupils in the 1st form (now Year 7) contained a bunch of talented sportsmen, several of whom won

representative honours with one becoming a county cricket captain and winning an England cap. Being a fiercely competitive Northerner I instilled into them the merits of giving 100% and also to be firm but totally fair in all their actions. One of my charges, however, who came from a nearby town with a different culture initially did not understand this and had the distinction of being the first boy to receive the sharp end of my slipper after he cheeked the opposition referee in our very first football match. We later became – and remain – good friends. Another working class boy from the same town, whom I had once asked the headmaster to sort out for misbehaviour in assembly, came to me when he left at 16 and said "Sir, would you give me a reference for a job please?" I was astounded. I had never actually taught him so asked why he had chosen me. He replied "Because you are firm but fair and always tell the truth!" I must admit to being rather humbled.

This incident came to mind several years later when, as deputy headmaster at an inner urban comprehensive school, I found myself being thanked by a leaving teacher I had previously ejected from my office. Let us say he was of foreign extraction with a fiery temper but clearly never held a grudge. On the first occasion he verbally lambasted me for not immediately disciplining a boy without first ascertaining the circumstances. On the second occasion he frog marched in a very thick 13 year old who had apparently thrown a rock at his front door at 3am that very morning. I also knew the boy had just stolen various items from a milk float down the road but while I was questioning him the teacher suddenly hit him in the face with his fist shouting "That's from me!" I didn't need to throw the teacher out a second time because he hurriedly exited without any persuasion. I quickly summed up the unexpected scenario, managed to restore order and somehow persuaded the wretch that justice had been done and that I would say no more about it. It worked but to be publicly thanked for all my support was a rather unexpected accolade and twist to the story. No more rocks were thrown at his front door either!

It was not the first or last time I sorted out someone else's problems but was not in the same league as when a former pupil came to see me and said "Sir, I need your help because I've committed an armed robbery!" He was a nice lad but not very bright and had simply flipped, armed himself with a metal bar and robbed the petrol station where he used to work! He and his girl friend had a new baby and were short of cash but, unsurprisingly, the girl cashier recognised him. I managed to persuade the judge to give him a suspended prison sentence and he later turned up at school to say "Thank you" and ask how he could apologise to the cashier who had refused to have anything more to do with him. We sat down and I helped him write a letter. I later did the same for another boy who had done something really stupid but came from a loving and supportive family. The result was another suspended sentence and it was gratifying to have the boy knock on my front door immediately afterwards to say "Thank you".

Boys will be boys and big boys are no different to small boys. While doing some after-school marking in only my second week of my first paid job I was startled by a frantic knocking on the window. I went to investigate and came face to face with a large, very wet sixth former with only the flimsiest of towels covering his modesty. "Have you got a key to the changing rooms, sir?" was his gasped request. Luckily for him, I had, and immediately opened up so he could be reunited with his clothes but how had he become detached from them in the first place? It turned out his mates had pinched them while he was in the shower and, in the process of chasing them they had locked him out. By the time I arrived they had fled – with the key!

On another occasion, during a summer camp when streaking was all the rage, a boy legged it out from the showers, across the playground and in through the front entrance. The following day his mate tried to upstage him and ran out on to the playing fields where he was discovered contemplating how he could climb back in through a window and streak across evening prayers – not a good idea and he was quickly ordered back from whence he came.

I doubt if such a prank would be laughed off today with the PC brigade having a field day. What happened to those years of innocence which might be best described as "the bare truth"? What indeed?

WHEELIES AND WHEELIE BINS

Why can't you get through to your child's school first thing in the morning? Answer: because it can't afford a full time secretary so the deputy head usually gets the chore – and what a chore it can be.

The day began at 6.45am as I was scoring the winning goal in the FA Cup Final. My alarm clock put paid to that and after going through my usual zombie routine of shower, cornflakes, coffee and cod liver oil tablet I was on my way. My wife staggered down the stairs to ask her usual "What time will you be back tonight?" to which I gave my usual response. "No idea. Depends on the curriculum meeting and football practice!"

It usually took 20 minutes to drive to school but this time it took 30 because as I was about to ascend a steep hill the windscreen suddenly misted up. Hastily switching off the engine I took a look under the bonnet but was surprised to find nothing obviously wrong so jumped back into the cockpit only to discover a cloud of steam leaking from under the dashboard. Knowing next to nothing about how cars work – the sign of a misspent youth when my main occupation in physics lessons was to pour alcohol on the bench and then set fire to it - I drove slowly on and reached school just as one of my slaves – I mean monitors – greeted me with a cheery "Morning sir. You're late today!" (see postscript)

En route I passed several children breaking the law on their early morning newspaper and milk rounds. How long had they been up? Would they stay awake in double maths that afternoon? Come to think of it what time did they go to bed? A survey I conducted some years earlier suggested many children rarely go up the wooden hill to Bedfordshire before midnight – unless they have a TV in their bedroom in which case they rarely emerged in the first place. Never mind, my immediate problem was fielding the usual round of stupid phone calls first thing on Monday morning, in particular which staff had a hangover and would ring in sick. You think I'm joking?

I narrowly missed George Wheeler (aptly named) doing wheelies on his bike in the playground but was then greeted by a sight straight out of Monty Python. School dustbins are large, very large and there, climbing out of one of them were two teenage boys. One I recognised was a bear of very little brain from Year 9 but the other was presumably his mate from another school – if he went to school at all. "What happened to you?" I heard myself asking to which I got a grumpy reply "Our mums locked us out so we had to sleep rough." Further investigation revealed they had not got home until 4am after doing goodness knows what, goodness knows where so I had some sympathy for one of the mothers, a young single mum who was trying hard to pay for her mistake some years earlier.

George had now pitched up on his bike to enjoy the fun so I enquired what he was doing at school at 8am when he often failed to turn up before 9. He explained how the family alarm clock had failed to go off and his dad, looking at his watch, decided it was already way past getting up time so pitched everyone out in double quick time, including himself. He was just pulling away when he noticed his neighbour's car was still parked so he checked his watch again, only to discover he had put it on upside down. Remember analogue watches? Don't think this could happen? Oh yes it can because I did it myself once.

As I made for the main entrance the headmaster emerged. "County Hall were on the phone last Friday evening. Mrs. Potter has been in to complain again. Says you called her son a liar, a thief and a cheat." How could I deny it? He was all of those things. (see second postscript). I thanked the head for the information and made a beeline for my study – or was it my office? Who cares? I was late so, not in the best frame of mine and vowing never to buy another French car, I fumbled in my pocket for the bunch of keys which weighed me down literally and metaphorically.

I could hear the phone. "That's the third time it's rung" said Jimmy Smith, my other chirpy early morning monitor who willingly ran errands in exchange for his weekly commendations which he collected like others collect postage stamps. I stumbled through the door, picked up the phone and heard a voice say "You a teacher?" "Well yes, I'm the deputy headmaster actually." "You'll do. My daughter's got diarrhoea. I knew you'd want to know" and promptly put the receiver down without identifying himself. Well that was comforting.

I often acted as surrogate doctor and nurse and it was not unusual to have four or five children sent in by their parents for a daily diagnosis. A similar number would also turn up not feeling well, usually from a "nedache" when I not always resisted the obvious temptation to inform the child they were not a donkey. Another regular affliction was a "bellyache" which I often suffered from too. Just occasionally something more serious turned up when I did my best to persuade the parents they needed professional advice. I also told staff they were not to send pupils to the medical room without telling me first. They rarely listened, though, and I once discovered a boy had actually kicked a hole in the wall because he was in so much pain from what was obviously appendicitis. It was not the first time I dialled 999 to discover there was no ambulance available. I insisted it was an emergency and so was grudgingly given a "sitting car" which required another adult to accompany the driver. In the past I had transported children directly to the casualty department myself but, after a teacher had an accident and his insurance company refused to pay up, the unions banned it so a frantic call to his family produced a willing grandfather who came to the rescue. Good job the boy's appendix hadn't burst or I would have had a possible death on my hands.

The phone rang again. "You a teacher?" I could almost have written the script "My daughter's got a detention after school tonight. Well she's not doing it see, 'cause she's got to pick her younger sister up, see?" I saw it very clearly. My attempts at trying to justify the detention fell on deaf ears and I knew I was

fighting a losing battle. What lay ahead for this girl was plain for everyone to see – except her short-sighted father. She was last heard of in court for shoplifting when all her father could offer in her defence was "I blame the school".

"Come in" I yelled to a knock on the door and was rewarded by two 11-year-old twins proudly holding a seagull which they had cornered on their way to school. "It's got a broken wing, sir. Can you stick it back together?" No I couldn't. Exit two crestfallen children who thought Sir was Superman or should that be Superglue?

The next phone call was from a teacher who patiently explained the colleague he usually gave a lift to had failed to turn up – again. It was bad news and we both knew it. The second teacher was suffering acute stress from the profession he once thought he had a vocation for and even at this stage it was clear he would never set foot in a classroom again. He never did.

The next call was from a teacher who had woken to find her house had been burgled while she was asleep. A call to the police at 6.30am revealed she was the 16th incident reported in her town since midnight. She would inevitably be late so I added her to the list of absentees for whom I had just five more minutes to arrange cover before the daily staff meeting.

The headmaster was called away just as I arrived so that left me in charge. I had just opened my mouth to welcome the silent collection of glum faces to another happy week at the fun factory when my words were drowned by the sound of breaking glass as a size 5 football illegally entered the staff room via a previously closed window. I rushed to the gaping hole to see four small boys legging it in the opposite direction but not quite fast enough. My stentorian voice – I was a Company Sergeant Major in my school cadet force who once bungled a parade of 400 cadets in front of a Brigadier-General after which the C.O.

never spoke to me again – boomed "Jones, Smith, Nelson and Quartermain come here – now!" They reluctantly skidded to a halt and returned rather more slowly than they had tried to depart. "Who kicked it?" "He did." "No I didn't." "Yes you did." "Well you told me to." "No I didn't." "Yes you did." Hmmmmm.

Staff briefing over I headed for the school office for a quick cup of coffee. I should have known better. "Just the man!" said the school secretary as I entered. "Have a look at this" and opened up a Tesco carrier bag to reveal a rather frightened white rabbit which had just been captured on the playground. My offer to take it to the kitchen because I was partial to rabbit pie was met with a snort of disapproval. "But it's frightened." I too would have been frightened after being chased round the playground by a howling group of 14-year-olds. It was obviously someone's pet so I released it back into the shrubbery from where I hope it found its way home. Rabbit pie would have to wait.

I returned indoors to hear the secretary say again "Just the man!" Now what? "Trouble in the music room. You're on emergency cover so can you go and release Jimmy Higgins who is stuck in a cupboard?" Switching on my blue flashing light I strode at a comfortable 5mph to confront what I knew was a wind up on the part of a small Irish boy who was a bit smarter than his young music teacher gave him credit for. The red-faced teacher was clearly uncomfortable but the class was strangely quiet as I marched in ready for battle, mainly because as I later discovered, they had laid bets on how long it would take me to get Jimmy out. They lost their wagers, however, because the conversation went something like this: "Jimmy. Come out of there at once." "Can't." "Yes you can." Can't, sir. I'm stuck." "No you're not. Come out now." "Can't!" "Yes you can but if you won't then I will drag you out." "Oh, all right then" said Jimmy as he uncoiled himself like a snake and emerged totally unscathed with a big grin on his face. He knew I meant it and would not have been too careful how hard I yanked him. "Report to my office after school." "But sir, it was only a joke." "Don't be late, Jimmy." "Yes, sir!"

It was the music teacher who had the last laugh, though, because a week later Jimmy, late as usual trundled in to find the class watching a colour costume drama on TV, Mozart's opera *Don Giovanni* no less. Jimmy was puzzled and said "'Ere, when was this filmed then?" to which the teacher replied "About 300 years ago". Jimmy thought for a moment then came out with "Naaaaa… you're pullin' me leg … it would have been in black and white." True!

PS The steam in the car turned out to be a design fault in the heating system which my mechanic discovered quite by chance and, as my vehicle was still under warranty, it was fixed for free.

PPS The very next morning, Mrs. Potter was waiting for me as I arrived. I feared the worst but was greeted by "Mr. Franklin, you're the only person who can help me. I'm at my wit's end with Gerald and if you don't tell me what to do I'm going to kill myself!" Well, well. Here was the same lady who had blackened my character with the authorities only a few days earlier. Hmmmm. (see incident in school gym – "Stinging Nettles and a Broken Leg").

SCHOOL ASSEMBLY

In my opinion morning assemblies are the lifeblood of every school because they serve three important functions:

1. They bring everyone together for an educational homily.
2. They provide a group *esprit de corps* (look it up in the dictionary) without which no school can operate effectively.
3. They give the perfect platform for disseminating information about school activities, successes, awards etc.

The headmaster, senior teacher and I took it in turns to lead assembly and vied with each other for the best illustration to make a particular point. Nobody ever remembers the details of a sermon or talk but a visual aid is likely to stick in the memory and remind one of at least something the speaker was trying to say.

I did pretty well with my illustrations but was completely upstaged one morning when the senior teacher refused to tell me what he was doing but asked to be given a grand entrance.

I duly obliged, following which I heard a flopping noise which, when it came into view, turned out to be a flat footed frogman. Actually, he looked more like something out of *Dr. Who* but I assumed it was my colleague about to do something unusual. He certainly did. Wearing a giant pair of flippers was not the best footwear to negotiate the short flight of steps to the platform and just as he reached the top he tripped and fell flat on his face – well on his face mask actually. Thinking this was part of the act the pupils cheered what they believed was a pretty good imitation of Norman Wisdom. The senior teacher, meanwhile, calmly picked himself up, removed his mask and started his talk. It was a successful assembly although quite what the moral was I really cannot remember. No doubt the senior teacher thought of "Look before you leap" or possibly "Remove flippers before ascending stairs".

It was the headmaster's prerogative to do the announcements and this day the school hockey team had trounced St. Trinian's, the football team had bounced St. Benedict's and the chess team had checkmated St. Matthew's. Now to the forthcoming production of *Oliver* and the head of music was holding auditions after school. "If you don't know who she is then Miss Green is standing on the back row in the pink." The thought of Miss Green standing in the nude was all too much and the senior teacher dissolved into an uncontrollable fit of giggles which he managed to stifle by pulling down his face mask. The joke was later explained to the headmaster who unfortunately compounded his gaffe a couple of weeks later by describing Mrs. Rhodes being "on the front row in the buff.' No face mask this time and it was all my colleagues and I could do to keep straight faces.

Guess who got the role of Bill Sykes in *Oliver*? It was my big moment and the piece de resistance was the song *My Name* in which Bill ends up daring the audience to mention his name.

On the first night I was building up to a rousing climax as I sang, louder and louder, "What is it? What is it? What is it? Myyyyyyy Nameeeeeee?" The silence and electric atmosphere was shattered by a little voice on the front row shouting out "Mr. Franklin!" to which another little voice responded with "No he isn't! He's my dad!" Out of the mouths and infants. I knew I shouldn't have invited my son and his chum along from their junior school.

Whenever a person appears on stage they should remember the old adage "Engage brain before opening mouth!" because there is always the chance of opening mouth and inserting one's proverbial foot. I always checked my flies before climbing the stage and never repeated the trick of a housemaster who jumped down from the platform and broke his ankle. I also once heard of a headmaster who managed to trip over a cable and fall straight into the school orchestra, demolishing the conductor en route. It cannot have done much for his dignity and mine came close to demolition at a prizegiving but was saved by the sharp-eyed chairman of governors neatly lifting away the glass of water trapped in the sleeve of my gown as I was handing over the books for distribution. If he had not spotted it just before it slid over the edge of the table then the guest of honour (the local bishop) and probably the headmaster too, would have experienced a sudden and serious case of soaking wet shoes and trousers. Explain that one away over drinks in the school library. By the way, do bishops still wear gaiters? I suspect not but must ask two former pupils of mine who now hold that honoured rank in the Church of England.

Back to school assembly. Many of my charges were not the brightest things on two legs so I took every opportunity to reward non-academic success. Our swimming pool was not huge but big enough for a potential fatal accident so my control over it was very strict. Even I, however, could not prevent one stupid idiot from jumping in the deep end, all six feet of it. He was an idiot because he could not swim and I was later told his older brother had once entered the school swimming gala and done exactly the same thing. It was only when he dived in that people realised he didn't know the difference between the doggie paddle and a doggie bowl! As Captain Mainwaring would say "Stupid boy!" As his younger brother splashed around shouting for help I told the nearest boy to fish him out and bring him to me, which he duly did. No need for panic and there wasn't any. I could have jumped in myself but what was the point of getting wet when the buffoon was only a few feet away with his head above water and his feet on the bottom?

Nevertheless, this was the perfect excuse for a certificate to be awarded in assembly and Jake Featherstone duly became an honoured recipient next morning. He was very proud, in fact just a little too proud as it turned out. Later that week my generosity to him was rewarded by the front page of the local paper with banner headlines screaming "Pupil rescues friend from drowning in school swimming pool!" Underneath was Jake holding his certificate aloft. Oh really! You would have thought he had swum the Channel so I was tempted to make a fuss but thought better of it because I might need the paper's support in the future. Meantime, you will not be surprised to learn that five years later Jake started a late night fire in a rubbish bin outside a huge store on a nearby business park which spread rapidly and burned down the whole expensive brand new premises. That also made the front page but without Jake holding a certificate.

Talking of firemen – or is it fire fighters these days – I returned to school one September to find a substantial section of the junior football pitch looking like *The Day of the Triffids*. The grass was 18 inches high and in need of a severe hair cut. Had the Martians invaded? Had the rural science teacher been testing a new fertiliser for his potatoes? Had the wretched doggy walkers been more anti-social than usual and each bought a Great Dane?

The answer was more mundane. It turned out the headmaster had given the local fire brigade permission to use the swimming pool during the hot summer holiday and, never having attended a course on swimming pools (which I had), invited them to empty the pool ready for the winter. That my dear Watson is something you never do because it is the pressure of the water which prevents the sides from falling in. No doubt the fire brigade had great fun sucking out millions of gallons of chlorinated water and dumping it on the nearest piece of ground which just happened to be my prize football pitch.

The pool was duly refilled at great expense, the grass was cut with extreme difficulty and normal service was resumed ... well sort of because one end of the pitch looked like the Centre Court at Wimbledon while the other looked more like the Sahara Desert. Hmmmm.

Shortly after the headmaster's second gaffe in assembly there was a sudden commotion as Jonathan Howard collapsed in a heap. As our trained first aider, Mrs. Hopkins leapt to the rescue and poor white-faced Jonathan suddenly found his feet unceremoniously hoisted into the air. It was in this undignified lowly position with his body and legs at a 90 degree angle that he watched the rest of the school depart around him. What had caused his demise? The headmaster's gaffe? No, as usual he had not eaten any breakfast. Hmmmm.

I had a free period next so as soon as everyone had departed I hotfooted it into the school kitchen where the head cook and I enjoyed a cup of coffee and a cheese roll.

What else might happen at the fun factory today? I did not have long to wait ....

THE WISDOM OF SOLOMON

Break time brought its usual array of nedaches and tummy aches plus assorted teachers complaining about pupils, and pupils complaining about teachers. Nothing new there then and doing my usual balancing act between a tightrope walker tiptoeing over the Niagara Falls and Houdini extricating himself from a comprehensive school milk churn buried at the bottom of the local river, I finally escaped and set off for my history lesson. Please remember I taught everything, anywhere, anytime, at the drop of a hat.

I was – inevitably – delayed en route. There is something about deputy heads which attract both teachers and pupils like a magnet. They are the fount of all knowledge, have the wisdom of Solomon and are able to solve everyone's problems at a stroke. The word "stroke" used to work well when corporal punishment was around because it cleared the air for everyone and meant fresh starts all round. Time was when a problem could be sorted almost immediately – not any more.

Mrs. Frobisher had lost her keys. Please could I let her into the classroom? I could and I did, only to discover the classroom was not actually locked in the first place, mainly because Mrs. Frobisher had left her keys on the desk. First problem solved. The sound of drilling and a loud yell then caused me to poke my nose round the library door where the librarian, putting up a new shelf, had just drilled straight through the wall into a computer on the other side. Not my problem – yet!

Turning the corner I found two Year 8 pupils knocking seven bells out of each other, with the rest of the class looking on enjoying the fight. "What on earth are you two playing at? Who's teaching you?" "You are, sir!" came a chorus of replies from the spectators. Oh yes, I nearly forgot. I got as far as saying "Get your books out, settle down and turn to chapter three. Today we're going to learn about …" but before I could finish the sentence the secretary rushed in.

"Come quick. There's a football team arrived from Kent for a tour match but I can't find the P.E. teacher." I knew nothing about any tour match so, muttering something about reading the chapter on Henry II which, I must confess, I had failed to read in advance myself and knew little more than the class at this stage, I set off in pursuit of the missing P.E. teacher. It did not take me long to locate him in the equipment store and ask what he knew about a team from Kent. Nothing at first then a train of thought crossed his mind, stopped and an idea got out.

"I did answer a letter about three months ago saying some school could come on a certain date but they never got back to me." Had he thought to check? No he hadn't but then organisation was never Charlie's best suit – in fact he never even owned a suit!

We set off for the school office at a brisk trot – me in the lead and Charlie close behind trying to keep up. When I met the track-suited teacher from Kent he greeted me with "Well, hello Mr. Franklin! Remember me?" Somewhat taken aback I replied "Surprise me!" He did for here was the captain of my Under 12 school team some 20 years previously, still smiling as he did all those years ago. I apologised profusely for someone else's misunderstanding at which both P.E. teachers magnanimously blamed themselves. That, however, did not solve the immediate crisis.

Solomon did a quick assessment of the situation and his wisdom came to the fore. "I will go round all the sixth form classes and see if I can raise a team to kick off in 30 minutes time." Before I did, however, I revisited my history class and threatened dire consequences if anyone let me down because the result would be an after-school detention. I was in such a hurry that I did not notice they were all smiling.

Biology, Geography and English sixth form classes were duly disrupted as I collected together enough pupils capable of kicking a football, who could nip home, get their kit and provide reasonable opposition against a touring team from Kent. You can guess what happened – we won the game and I didn't know whether to laugh or cry. Fortunately, my former pupil accepted the result with good grace. Should I strangle Charlie? Better not, we might need him in the future – suit or no suit.

Back to my class and as I entered I was aware of stifled giggles. "What's so funny? I told you to get on with the lesson!"

Again threatening a detention I put on my serious face but had it completely wiped off by a boy on the back row saying "Please sir. If you put us all in detention, will Miss Stewart have to do it as well?" Miss Stewart? She was a teacher. Then the penny dropped because there, sitting on the front row dressed as a naughty schoolboy complete with ragged tie and school cap at a jaunty angle was the aforesaid Miss Stewart with a huge grin on her face. .

Whose idea was it to swap a pupil with a teacher and see what happened? Mine! Feeling distinctly hoisted with my own petard I let my guard down and joined in the joke. No, Miss Stewart would not have to join the detention and I complimented the class on their admirable restraint under trying circumstances – well they were trying – whichever way you look at it!

Once, on a deputy head's residential weekend course we were asked to speak about an initiative we had successfully introduced. My reply took everyone by surprise. Protocol and good manners could not be taken for granted in my inner-urban school so I announced in assembly that all pupils were expected to hold the door open for teachers but the teachers must say "Thank you" in return. Any teacher failing to do so could be reported to me. I was soon inundated with complaints, one of which was against the headmaster! Then I was really caught out. "Yes Jimmy?" "I want to report a teacher who failed to say 'thank you'" "Yes Jimmy?" "You, sir!" What? Could this be true? Jimmy then added with a chuckle " ... but you didn't see me, sir, 'cause I was 'iding behind the door!"

On another occasion when visiting my local bank I jokingly said to a young man who had made a spelling mistake "Well I obviously didn't teach you." Back came his swift reply "Well actually Mr. Franklin …" He had been in Year 7 when I left and, truth to tell, I did not remember him at all – but he had remembered me. Whoops! We both burst out laughing.

Following my disrupted history lesson it was time to switch to geography. I arrived ten minutes later having just calmed down a distraught parent in the school office who had arrived just as I was talking to a school inspector about the music lesson I had taken the previous week, in a physics lab overseen by an HMI qualified in drama. It was certainly dramatic all right – as was this short interview because as the wailing mother burst through one door so the inspector exited quickly through the other. Typical! It was Mrs. Greenhalgh who simply could not cope with her two errant sons. Her husband had long since departed the scene and I had met both her sons in a previous interesting incarnation.

While supervising my own three small children in the local swimming pool, two of whom had not yet learnt to swim properly, I noticed two boys fall off the large float in the middle and get into difficulty. Handing my youngest child to my oldest, I promptly fished the two boys out, gasping for breath (the boys, not me) and suggested they went to get changed and tell their parents of their narrow escape. Where was the life guard? Down the other end of the pool and had obviously not witnessed the incident.

I then rescued my own children who had also got into difficulty before heading for the changing rooms about 20 minutes later. Here, much to my surprise, I came across the same two boys I had just rescued (they must have been about 7 or 8 years old), running around, stark naked, hitting each other with their towels and yelling like banshees. I immediately said to the only adult present "You've got a handful there!" to which he replied "They're nothing to do with me and they've been at it for 20 minutes!"

It was at this point that father arrived on the scene and started yelling at them for being late. I quietly informed him I had just rescued them from drowning at which point he erupted a second time and screamed "That's it! They're not coming again!" before turning on his heels and departing, leaving his two sons to carry on their Tweedledum and Tweedledee acts of orchestrated violence. It would have been nice if he had thanked me but, as I later discovered, he was already on the verge of walking out of the family home. So positive was I that the two boys would eventually end up at my school that I asked their names. I was right and here was mother, five years later, almost literally crying on my shoulder in the school office. I often wonder what happened to the boys. More than likely they joined the Army.

Arriving at my class I discovered clandestine operations going on in a corner which were hastily covered up as I entered. "Why haven't you got your exercise books out?" "Please sir, you took them in last week. You said you hadn't marked them!" Quite right, I hadn't marked them for at least three weeks and they were sitting in my office at the other end of school. Yikes! Breaking all my own rules I entrusted my huge bunch of keys to the most reliable girl in the class who strutted off as pleased as Punch.

Meantime "What's happened to the Ordnance Survey maps?" "Please sir, Matthew Withers is away." "Well what about his deputy?" "He's away too, sir!" I might have known. It never occurred to anyone to show a bit of initiative. On second thoughts perhaps they were sharper than I gave them credit for as I seem to remember a similar scenario when I was at school. Hmmmm.

I despatched two pupils to collect the maps from the history room. I never quite worked out why they were stored there but as I was teaching geography in a French room it hardly mattered. Once upon a time I had my own room but that was once upon a time which, as everyone knows, is a very long time ago.

The maps duly arrived and so did the exercise books, all across the classroom floor as my trusty slave made a spectacular entry, tripping flat on her face and neatly distributing the books in all directions. "Did you have any trouble locking my door, Jane?" She looked up at me from her prone position in total amazement and said "But sir, you only asked me to open the door not close it!"

My attempts to get the lesson going were then thwarted a second time. "Settle down and find Southampton on your map and answer the first five questions in the book." Not too difficult I thought but I was wrong. After about 30 seconds three hands went up accompanied by puzzled faces. "What's the matter? Don't you understand plain English?"

"I can't find Southampton on my map, sir." "Neither can I." "Nor me, sir." These were the brightest members of the class, the rest having yet to establish which way up the map went. I was beginning to lose patience when I noticed two red faced pupils quietly having hysterics in the corner. "What's so funny you two?"

"Please sir, we thought you said get the Northampton maps!" Well, it was close.

We managed to survive the rest of the lesson and soon it was time for lunch. What happened next, however, was undoubtedly the most serious incident I dealt with during the whole of my teaching career ….

BEANS AND CHIPS PLEASE!

Breaking my own rules yet again, I dismissed my class a couple of minutes early and made for the dining hall where I was, as usual, on duty. The secret was to get there ahead of the hungry hordes requesting their beans and chips. No healthy eating here, it was what the troops wanted and what their parents demanded.

The splendid kitchen staff worked miracles but even they couldn't convince this lot that leaf mould and lettuce was preferable to bangers and beefburgers. Serving cabbage and cucumber to our local natives was a bit like serving ice cream to the Eskimos. One Christmas I noticed a couple of boys produce free meal tickets who were clearly not entitled to them.

"Where did you get these?" was greeted by "We bought them cut price from the Scholes twins who don't like turkey!" The Mafia had nothing on these two crooks but I soon put a stop to their black market trade in beans and chips.

The queue was already building up when I arrived and I knew my query as to how they got there early would be a waste of time. "We've come from P.E. sir. We forgot our kit so got out early." They always seemed to forget their kit and always somehow managed to get away with it, mainly because sanctions prove ineffective when parents don't care. "Well stop pushing and shoving. You'll get there in the end." As I turned my back so the queue collapsed in a heap. "Serves you jolly well right" was my most unworthy thought.

The bell went and before you could say "Grub up" little ants swarmed in from everywhere, intent on demolishing everything in their path, especially the food. Alice, the head cook, had already prepared her usual mountain of chips and spent the next 45 minutes frantically trying to keep pace with demand. "Beans and chips" was invariably followed by "Beans and chips" occasionally punctuated by "Sausage, beans and chips". One polite youngster actually said "Please" and was rewarded by a few extra chips on his plate. Well done the kitchen staff.

A squeal of protest suddenly shattered the peace and we all looked round to find a first former being strangled by a sixth former. "He poured salt all over my dinner" said the bigger of the two. "No I didn't ..." gasped the smaller urchin as he surfaced for air, " .... it was Tommy Roberts". I imagine they were probably both in it up to their necks – well one of them certainly was – but I diffused the situation and when everything had calmed down, stuck my head round the kitchen door and said "Fish fingers, peas and potatoes please" to which Christine, with a pained expression replied "Sorry luv, they're off. How about beans and chips?"

No sooner had I sat down again when in trooped three small boys, one of whom was distinctly the wrong colour. His jacket was grey and so was his tear-stained face. "I've got a nedache!" Not another donkey. Actually, this one was different because it transpired one of the other two had accidentally kicked his football into a large dustbin and Neddy had overbalanced when trying to get it out and fallen in head first. No wonder he had a nedache and no wonder he was not exactly smelling of roses. I administered tender loving care and then, in one of my playful moods, said "Would you like a cyanide capsule?" "Yes please!" was not quite the answer I had in mind so he settled for a boiled sweet instead and went off to resume his game of footy in the playground.

Lady teachers don't normally run but this one did. "Quick. James Cavanagh has just told me Roger Jones has fallen through the ice on the balancing pond!" I dialled 999 and ran to the pond half a mile away. By the time I arrived the fire brigade, whose HQ was literally just round the corner, were packing up. "False alarm mate" was all the driver could say. I didn't know whether to laugh or cry but a later summons for Roger Jones revealed he had indeed gone through the ice but not in the middle, as his wet trousers up to his knees testified. I gave him an ear bashing for breaking bounds at lunchtime at which he hung his head before straightening up with a grin and handing me a battered envelope saying "Happy Christmas, sir. Here's your card!"

What happened next, however, was horrendous. I never knew the secretary could move so fast but she ran into the dining hall at breakneck speed as I was shovelling down my beans and chips while chatting to the headmaster. "Emergency!" she gasped "A boy's tried to kill himself by swallowing a bottle of bleach!" A shiver went down my spine and does so again now as I write these words. I was off like a bullet from a gun to find the 14 year old vomiting on the office floor. I had done first aid courses but this was different so, almost without thinking, I hastily filled an empty milk bottle with water and ordered him to drink as much as he could, as fast as he could. I then dialled 999 and called an ambulance, after which the headmaster strolled in and said "If it was me I would have given him milk." I could have happily given *him* a bottle of milk but not to drink!

It transpired the boy's girl friend had jilted him and this was his immediate but unthinking response. I managed to track his father down at work by insisting it was a matter of life and death and asking him to go down to casualty at once. Happily, the boy's vomiting and my prompt action saved the day but it was not an event I would wish to repeat. Get this, however, within weeks I was replaced as the school first aider by the aforesaid secretary because she had attended a more up to date course than me. There's reward for you ....

BAITHOVEN AND BARK

I must have been the only music teacher in the country who couldn't play a musical instrument – yes really! Like all deputy heads I got lumbered with what was left over on the timetable and during my career I taught no fewer than ten different subjects, but music …? Well actually I enjoy music and later became the music editor of a significant international magazine … but I digress.

Music has come a long way since I sat on the back row of our second form school music lessons (no Year 8 when I was at school) singing "Do you ken John Peel". Actually we didn't ken *John Peel* and I squirm at the alternative version which me and my extremely vulgar chums bellowed out in competition with

the goody goodies on the front row. I think the music teacher was deaf but not too deaf to bang his hands down on the keys and shout "You boys on the back row. You're not singing the right words! I can tell by your mouths." It was a good job he couldn't lip read because if he could we would have deservedly received six of the best. I blush when I think about it! If it was Eric Morecambe he might have answered "We're singing all the right words – but not necessarily in the right order!"

Never mind, time moves on and the children in my music lessons were soon thrilling to the sounds of Louis Armstrong and his Hot Five, and Jelly Roll Morton and his Red Hot Peppers. Never heard of them? Shame on you because they were the pick of the late-1920s American jazz scene which I discovered during my teens. The seed was sown by a young student teacher who turned up one day with some old 78 rpm records which he played for us on a wind-up gramophone. I went up to him afterwards and said I liked them whereupon – get this – he gave them to me. What is more, I still have them and in recent years have re-recorded them on the CD label which I organise. I wish I could have thanked him for his generosity.

Fast forwards five years to the sixth form and the same poor music teacher being lumbered with a group of arrogant 16 year olds (one of whom is now a director of a famous football club) who took great delight in baiting him. The aforesaid director, who also laid out several opposition goalkeepers each year in his starring role as 1st XI centre forward (strikers had yet to be invented), took extra delight in pretending to enjoy the pulsating last part of the 3rd movement of Tchaikovsky's *Pathetique Symphony*, at which the teacher would smile and play it again. I am not sure if he ever twigged he was being made a fool of but, just as on the football field where I was the goalkeeper, I watched the antics from a safe distance. Once, when his friend, who was actually a fine trumpeter, overstepped the mark the poor old teacher flipped and attacked him. Silence ensued after which the startled pupil could only whisper "You shouldn't have done that sir!" He shouldn't and everyone knew it but who could blame him. We were musical bear baiters and he was the bear.

Then it happened .... one day he played a piece of music which I recognised and was instantly hooked. No more messing about. The revelation was the opening of the dramatic 3rd movement of Dvorak's *7th Symphony* which was the introductory theme to Walter Scott's novel *Redgauntlet* which had just been screened on television. To the sound of this great music, in the opening sequence a horseman galloped madly across the Solway Firth and when I later met the actor/horseman on a school cruise he owned up to being absolutely terrified of horses! I had suddenly discovered serious music and I liked it. A lifetime of musical appreciation followed and I only wish I could have thanked the man who inadvertently started me off. If only he had known he had been a success and not a failure.

Back to my class at school. At the time I may not have known a basset horn from a treble clef but I knew what I liked. The fact that my pupils knew a great deal less than me, however, was perfectly illustrated when I decided to quell a riot in the English room next door. Before I departed I invited my charges to write ten famous composers on the blackboard (whiteboards had yet to be invented).

Having flexed my muscles and disciplined several clowns next door - and I include the teacher in that description – I returned to see what they had come up with. The results were interesting if not terribly accurate.

Top of the pops was Baithoven (clearly a fisherman); followed at number 2 by Bark (obviously a lumberjack); number 3 was

Handle (must be a crank); with Crokoskey (Tchaikovsky) in 4th place. Number 5 had me beaten for some time though. Was Sarsons the 19th Century fish and chip shop owner who invented malt vinegar? Then the penny dropped – they meant Saint-Saens!

Number 6 was Paul McCartney who was actually a composer of sorts although apparently cannot read music (like me) but as for Liberace, Nigel Kennedy, the Rolling Stones and Status Quo I had my doubts.

I congratulated them on their efforts and celebrated with a full blown version of Jelly Roll Morton's all time classic *Doctor Jazz*. I was about to clip Jimmy Smith round the ear when I realised he was tapping his ruler in time to the beat and trying to emulate Jell Roll's throaty Creole singing. Perhaps he had experienced one of those life changing moments as I had 30 years before. Why not? It happened to me and it could happen to anyone with the realisation there is more to music than Madonna or Michael Jackson.

The following year I knew I had cracked it as far as music lessons were concerned and can do no better than quote the following extract from a webpage I wrote about the composer Phyllis Tate:

"One of the author's favourite pieces is the delightful four-movement suite *London Fields*, commissioned for the BBC Light Music Festival in 1958. With the help of a privately recorded performance he used it to introduce a class of inner-urban very academically limited boys to music more serious than the contemporary pop to which they were accustomed. As each of the movements unfolded, so the children were invited to sketch what came into their minds. *Springtime at Kew* evoked daffodils and crocuses; *The Maze at Hampton Court* produced all kinds of curly-wurly shapes; *St. James' Park – a Lakeside Reverie* resulted in ducks and swans swimming a-plenty while the grand finale, *Hampstead Heath – Rondo for Roundabouts* brought forth all manner of helter-skelters, dodgem cars, candy floss, toffee apples and the like. The icing on the cake came after the fourth week when a small boy approached the teacher at the end of the lesson and said "Please sir, I like this music. Can you do a recording for me?" He got his recording and for all I know he is, like me, still playing it."

Follow that! I enjoyed teaching music and have since got to know several influential people in the music profession whose blushes I will spare by not naming them!

PS I learnt only recently that the head of music deliberately used to play both jazz and English symphonies very loudly to his class when he knew I was in my office down the corridor with bets taken as to how long it would take me to arrive and identify the piece in question. True – even if it took him another 20 years to own up!

STINGING NETTLES AND A BROKEN LEG

The afternoon bell sounded and, with a double free period, I was looking forward to marking the geography books which had been burning a hole in my desk for several days. Don't ever believe a teacher who claims to mark their books regularly or faithfully corrects every mistake. It doesn't happen – unless they never go to bed. I was ten minutes into my red biro scribbling when ....

A loud bang on the door usually meant trouble and I was not to be disappointed. There stood George, the assistant P.E. teacher with a boy who looked more like Herman Munster. His face, arms, and legs and, as I quickly discovered, most of his torso were covered in blisters. Fearing bubonic plague or an outbreak of Frankenstein I began to look for the emergency number of the National Inspector of Health. The explanation, however, turned out to be more mundane. At the start of the cross country run his mates had apparently rolled him over several times in some nettles – just for a laugh you understand. The results were appalling.

Dr. Kildare (that shows my age) immediately ordered George to put the boy in a cold shower while I organised his mates – probably ex-mates by now – to go and collect as many dock leaves as they could find. Personally, I wouldn't know a dock leaf from a dandelion but they said they did and, amazingly, because they were mainly boys from the local council estate, came back with several armfuls which George and I gently dabbed on the patient. Equally amazingly, they worked! Bubonic plague avoided – the country saved – back to my marking. Some hopes!

Within another five minutes came a second bang on the door. Mrs. Freeman was standing there not at all happy with two small second-formers who had just turned up late for her lesson looking like they had been dragged through a bog backwards. They had – by each other! Experience told me they had done it deliberately because they fancied the afternoon off. "You'll have to send us home to change, sir." "Oh I will, will I?" No 13-year-old tells me what to do and when there were two obviously in cahoots it was quite clear to me – although not to Mrs. Freeman – that they had manufactured the situation deliberately. Their blazers were caked in mud, as were their shoes, socks, trousers and shirt. Now what?

I rang George who was just putting the final polish and shine on Frankenstein and told him he had two more customers for the cold shower. In the meantime I would arrange some emergency clothing. The urchins obviously thought they could dodge games because it was chucking it down outside which they had just proved quite conclusively by dragging each other through the largest and muddiest puddle they could find. Well two could play at that game and I always had Plan B ready for just such a situation. Lost property could be very useful.

If you have seen the film *Kes* then you will know exactly what happened next. I sought out the most ill fitting P.E. kit I could find and made the two shivering urchins put them on. They emerged looking more like a cross between Michelin Man and a clown with size 20 shoes. I also wrote a note to their parents explaining exactly how their offspring had arrived home looking like a tramp although I doubt if they ever bothered to hand the message over. Quite what the parents thought I never discovered because I never heard any more about it.

I just had time to mark a few more books before the bell reminded me I was on games – second year games where Michelin Man and Coco the Clown were about to put in an appearance. Their elaborate ploy to dodge games had failed miserably – you will have worked out by now that they had also deliberately left their kit at home – and in any event Charlie and George, i.e. the PE Department, decided it would be better to keep everyone indoors and spare the playing fields from further destruction by imbecilic vandals wearing size 5 trainers.

Charlie took centre stage while George and I kept a wary eye on the sidelines. Everything was going well until a piggy back race went spectacularly wrong. A horse stumbled over Becher's Brook and his jockey took a graceful airborne header before landing with a clump. At first he giggled so I said "Stop messing about and get up." He tried but found he couldn't at which it was immediately obvious (to me at least) that something was seriously wrong – just as it had been when a batsman neatly removed both the wicketkeeper's top front teeth when he mistimed a sweep to leg during the summer term. On that occasion I immediately rang the dentist while his mate scooped up the teeth from the pitch. Within 30 minutes they were back in his mouth. Absolutely true!

I raced over, gently picked up the casualty, carried him back to the bench where a sudden rapid swelling made it abundantly clear he had broken his leg. Leaving George in charge of this latest patient, I dialled 999 and requested an ambulance. It duly arrived and took away the amazingly amenable lad but not before I assured him I would notify his family. They weren't on the phone so I wrote another note and despatched it via Wells Fargo – well his next door neighbour actually – explaining exactly what had happened and how I had dealt with the situation. I failed to mention I was not in charge, however, which turned out to be a mistake – a big mistake.

I felt quite pleased with myself. I had been able to help someone in need and had done everything required in an emergency. Well not quite it seemed because two days later County Hall rang to say the boy's stepfather had lodged a complaint for negligence against me personally. Me? I wasn't even in charge of the lesson! The boy was a nice lad but his stepfather wasn't. I pleaded my case with the Chief Education Officer – whom I knew from a previous school – to which he replied "There is no point in defending the case. It's cheaper for us to make an ex-gratia payment to the stepfather because it would cost us more to take him to court and find he has no money to pay our substantial costs when we win!" Well, that's it then – head he wins, tails we lose. I still smoulder at the injustice more than 30 years later.

You will be pleased to know that Michelin Man and Coco the Clown proved to be the centre of attraction and I took particular satisfaction in overhearing one of their chums gloatingly whisper to them "Told you you'd never get away with it!"

INTERNATIONAL SPORTING SUCCESS

The bell went for the end of school by which time I was cunningly concealed overlooking the bike sheds to see who picked up the stolen bike which the owner had spotted. I did not have long to wait, made a citizen's arrest (well a deputy head's arrest) and invited the local constabulary to interview the culprit. At first he denied his guilt then gave himself away by trying to run out of the door. Game, set and match.

Meanwhile, back on the football field my team were having fun with their after-school practice – all except one who informed me he didn't want to play for the school any more but was quite happy to watch from the touch line. This did not please me at all so I despatched him pronto, adding he would not be welcome at my evening youth club footballing activity later that evening. Amazingly, he turned up and could see nothing wrong. I pointed out it was my activity in my own time and that I could accept or deny access to whoever I wanted. If he wasn't prepared to support me and the school team then he could hardly be expected to use the school facilities whenever he chose outside school hours.

Even more amazingly, within 15 minutes he was back accompanied by his mother! She obviously thought her son could do what he liked as well but soon found out he couldn't and went home more than a little miffed. Surprisingly, this lad went on to play rugby for a top class team, as did two others from his year, none of whom was a first choice for the school football team. Unfortunately, this was not true of another really nice boy who was superb at everything and would surely have gone higher had his first class rugby career not been ruined by a serious knee injury.

On my way home I often met a fourth boy who did make the big time, albeit at schoolboy level. His rugby training for an older team took place at the same time as my football but he alone used to stay on and practise his kicking before having a shower while the rest of his team trooped off home in their dirty kit. Their coach was older than me and I never questioned his style but I never allowed my charges to disappear like that, fully believing that *esprit de corps* begins and ends in the changing room.

The boy lived near me and could easily have walked home so the first time I met him waiting at the bus stop I asked him why. His response is engraved on my memory: "Sir, I'm just too tired." At the age of 14 he was put forward for the County trials from where he proceeded to the South West then South of England. When he was called up for the full England trial he came to me bursting with pride and said "Sir, it's great to have got this far but there will be others better than me."

I told him in no uncertain manner that everyone there would be thinking the same thing but as long as he did his best it really did not matter whether he got selected or not. Nobody was more pleased than me, therefore, when he was chosen to play full back for England Under 15s versus Italy at Twickenham, followed by a European tour. It could not have happened to a nicer person and I organised a coach load of supporters to see him tread the hallowed turf in London. I later photographed him in his England kit and I hope the picture still holds pride of place in the school foyer.

One lad (not from my own school) actually made the full England rugby team but only ever once played for my district football team. At the age of 11 his language was appalling and after hearing him in the back of the minibus I was driving to a match, I silently vowed he would never play for me again. He never did but his fanatical rugby-playing headmaster single-handedly turned him around from what locals called "a fat lard" into a pleasant young man who made the very highest

grade. Now that's what I call a teacher and I hope his pupil realised just how much he owed his England career to his mentor.

Meanwhile, back in the school gym we always played "skins v. shirts" in a well-rehearsed procedure which saw eight teams play seven fixtures in less than an hour - 28 matches in all at an average of around 1½ minutes each, leaving plenty of time for a final game of rumbustious British Bulldog. It was great entertainment for everyone and the entry fee of 5p paid for various other internal youth activities which I ran in my spare time.

The only snag, however, was that boys occasionally picked up the wrong shirt, which was easy to do when everyone in those days supported either Liverpool or Manchester United. One father came storming into school the following day protesting his son had taken the wrong kit home and that his particular shirt had been bought on a trip to Anfield. Unfortunately for everyone, including me, several others owned an identical Liverpool shirt so quite how he knew he had the wrong one I don't know. Exhaustive investigations failed to turn up the missing item so perhaps in future he made sure his son's name was in his kit – which was the school rule anyway.

Only those who love football - which does not include my wife - can understand why people travel the country to watch it. As Chairman and Secretary of my local District F.A. I organised various cups and competitions right across the Midlands and South of England. There were many highlights including winning in a large Welsh city on a former old First Division ground, then demolishing a top team from London at home before losing an English Schools quarter-final on a freezing cold night right underneath the M25 in London. My team once even beat Portsmouth Academy in a cup final.

The vast majority of boys and parents were proud to represent their District but not all (see also chapter on Failures). I could never resist a challenge so when a fellow footballing enthusiast I met on a school cruise invited me to take two teams from my district to the wilds of the Northamptonshire-Lincolnshire border I could not refuse. We took both school minibuses, won both matches and enjoyed their hospitality but on the Monday my headmaster received a complaint from a motorist who phoned to say he had been driving along the M5 when one of our team had dropped his trousers and mooned out of the minibus window. Mooning is a euphemism for baring one's buttocks and started in America many years ago before becoming popular in Britain via a late night TV show circa 1980. My colleague and I knew immediately who was responsible, a boy from a rival school whose background was less than satisfactory. Happily, for me at least, he was travelling in the other minibus so I felt a little less annoyed. A phone call to his headmaster ensued but much worse occurred the following year when the boy's younger brother, a nice lad, was tackled in a local derby match and fell over. It was not a foul and no big deal but what happened next beggars belief. As I followed the ball I heard a boy screaming "Get off him, dad!" The game immediately ground to a halt and all eyes were transfixed on a father who had pinned an opposition 14-year-old to the ground and was punching him in the head. His son was absolutely distraught while the referee raced across and pulled the man off his unfortunate victim. I was aghast but let the officials decide what to do next. Frankly, I felt he was lucky to escape police action which is surely what would have happened today – but not then. A mild reprimand from the same headmaster was all that followed! All the man could say in his defence was "He tackled my son!" You really couldn't make it up because in those days such an action was totally unbelievable. Sadly, not any more.

We enjoyed many school sporting trips for which I never claimed a penny, neither did I ever claim expenses or a fee for hundreds of matches I refereed. I did it for fun and because I enjoyed the company of like-minded children and adults. Occasionally a parent would offer a word of thanks and, very occasionally, so would a boy. I even briefly flirted (not the right word if taken out of context) with girls football, most of whom were also appreciative because nobody else on the staff was interested. One of their number, on hearing I would be leaving the school, came to me in some distress and asked "It's not true that you're leaving sir, is it?" I said it was and that I had been head-hunted by another school at which she stamped her foot and shouted very angrily "That's it then!" before storming off down the corridor. She never spoke to me again. What it is to be appreciated without knowing it!

Perhaps the ultimate accolade, however, was being invited to organise an Under 18 Schoolboy International between England and Wales. It was a great occasion and played in the best of spirits. I wrote to all the high profile footballing pundits and asked for a comment for the match programme. Astonishingly, by return of post came letters from both Gary Lineker and Graham Taylor, England's centre forward and manager respectively, together with specific comments and photographs. I was hugely impressed and have been big fans of theirs ever since. Others came in late, including goalkeeper Peter Shilton and a phone call the weekend before the match (!) from the England assistant manager, Laurie McMenemy. Other famous names never replied but I had already been forewarned that certain people, despite their high public persona, were both unreliable and arrogant and were unlikely to help.

Definitely not among the latter was Bobby Robson, in my opinion the finest ever England manager. A teaching colleague, a Football League linesman, once took me to a cup replay between Portsmouth and Fulham, who at the time were bottom of the old 1st Division (the equivalent of today's Premier League). Portsmouth, a Second Division team, won 1-0 and as I was waiting under the stand for my colleague to change, out came the Fulham team to face the press. First up was Johnny Haynes who, at £100 a week, was the highest paid player in the country. "What did he think?" asked the press. Haynes was not bothered because he was a top earner. Also there was Alan Clarke, later of Leicester City, Leeds and England but last out was Bobby Robson on whom the media vultures swooped. "Are you going to get the sack?" His reply was a classic and showed the enormous stature of the man …. "Listen lads. I asked my boys to give me 100% effort out there tonight. They did and so I have no complaints. If I get the sack then so be it!" He received his cards not long afterwards together with his chief coach, Roy McCrohan who just happened to be in charge of the FA Coaching Badge I was attending. When he arrived the following week there was an uneasy silence which he broke with "Don't worry about me and Bobby, another job will come along soon". It did and the rest is history. Robson inspired his charges with optimism and I hope I did the same.

My reward for organising this schoolboy international was an invitation to dinner at Wembley prior to a televised schoolboy international between England and Germany where I rubbed shoulders with the former England coach Sir Walter Winterbottom, and the guest of honour, the great Sir Stanley Mathews. What a gentleman and I will leave the last words to him. When asked in a televised post-match interview to outline his career he responded with: "Let's not talk about me. It's their day so let's talk about the boys." That, ladies and gentleman, was a true sportsman speaking.

THE RUMBLING HIPPOPOTAMUS

It was 2pm and I was lost in thought when my phone rang. "Are you sitting comfortably?" It was the secretary in the school office and I just knew there was trouble brewing. "Mr. Briggs is here and wants to see you."

Oh no, not the dreaded Mr. Briggs! His son Geoffrey was, for want of a better expression, a large first year pupil. Well no, not really. Geoffrey was huge – enormous in fact. He was more like a cross between a rhinoceros and a hippopotamus but rather more thick-skinned with a small brain at the end of his horn. His father was even more formidable with a skin like the outer plating of a battleship – and no brain whatsoever. It could be a

difficult interview and I had a nasty suspicion I knew what it was going to be about.

It had all started when the phone rang at 8am the previous Friday morning. Charlie, the head of PE, admitted that his intestines and last night's red hot Indian cuisine had not ended up on the same wavelength and that he needed to stay within a short distance of the smallest room in the house. Please could someone take his lessons? Hmmmm.

I managed to cover them all apart from period 2 for which, according to the timetable, there were no spare teachers and no spare rooms or gymnasium. Then a horrible realisation dawned on me. There was a spare teacher – me!

"We're not going outside are we, sir? It's chucking it down!" "Tough because there's no alternative. What are you? A snivelling bunch of whimps?" That did it. Not only were we going outside, we were going to jolly well enjoy it. Well I was because I had my training top and bottoms over the top of my track suit, and my large anorak on top of that.

The keen ones ploughed through the mud trying to play football on what resembled a Chinese paddy field during the monsoon season. Not every boy thought it was fun though, and

I wondered what to do with the conscientious objectors when I had an idea. Before I knew it I had uttered the fateful words "Any boy who doesn't get muddy by the end of the lesson will be dropped in a puddle" - and there were plenty to choose from. That ought to provoke a response. It did!

Before you could say "David Beckham" the game of football ceased and the pitch was turned into a war zone as players turned into hippopotamuses – or should that be hippopotami - with mud flying everywhere.

It occurred to me "whataclotami" if parents complained. That was unlikely, however, because the boys and their muddy kit could all be cleaned off in the showers. The only parent who might not see the funny side was the father of Geoffrey Briggs but he was safely ensconced in the changing rooms with his usual excuse note (probably forged by his older brother who was even bigger) complaining of an in-growing toe nail (more like an in-growing brain if you ask me) – at least that is where he was supposed to be.

I'm sure you can guess what happened next. No self-respecting hippopotamus can resist a mud bath and hearing the squeals of delight from the rest of the class he emerged from his hiding place and waddled straight into the middle of the fight – still wearing his school uniform.

I spotted him too late! What would his dad say? Perhaps Geoffrey might tell him the truth? Perhaps hippopotamuses might fly? Frankly, I was surprised I hadn't heard from dad before but he apparently did not find out until Saturday morning and I am ex-directory (I had to be in my job) and this was his first opportunity to track me down.

Geoffrey had not told him the truth (I knew hippopotamuses couldn't fly) and had spun a cock and bull story about other boys attacking him – at my suggestion – as they came off the football pitch. Now what?

I know one can't reason with an unreasonable person but have you ever tried reasoning with an unreasonable hippopotamus? Before I had a chance to explain, the enraged animal threw his son's blazer at me and demanded I wash it. I dodged the still soggy missile and politely declined. He shouted at me again – more like a snort really – but I stood my ground and thought quickly – while I was still on my feet – how I could prevent this rampaging animal from charging down the corridor pursuing a hapless deputy head. In a flash of inspiration I played what I hoped and prayed would be my trump card.

"If you don't leave the safari park (I mean school) then I will call the game wardens (I mean police)." I tried to sound convincing as I made a dignified exit into the school office where I quickly took refuge with the secretary behind a locked door. I emerged, very cautiously, five minutes later only to find the hippo still scraping his feet in the corridor. Throwing caution to the wind before the hippo threw me into the wind I took him by the horns (I know hippos don't have horns but just pretend they do while I finish the story) and calmly announced "The police are on their way!"

It wasn't true because I hadn't rung them but it did the trick. I got the distinct impression this particular hippo had met the game wardens before and was not anxious to cross their path again. I wonder why? Before you could say "David Attenborough" he rumbled through the front door of the safari park (I mean school) and disappeared – not quite in a cloud of smoke but I swear the tarmac bounced up and down as he fled.

Strangely, I never heard another word. Maybe the poachers bagged him before he reached the end of the drive? Maybe Geoffrey told him the truth? I never found out but next time I saw Geoffrey – with his PE kit would you believe – I was reminded of the phrase "Like father, like son". In about 25 years time it would be some other poor deputy head's turn to tame an unhappy hippo.

LET THE TRAIN TAKE THE STRAIN

As I am something of a railway buff my study is packed with railway books of all kinds – I even have three redundant concrete gradient and mile posts plus a set of signals in my back garden. My experiences of trains with school groups, however, was not always satisfactory. When I tried to arrange a group reservation from London to Cornwall I ended up with a special train shared with another camp. It was also agreed that arrangements would be made for the return journey but when I rang to check this some time later I was told they knew nothing about it. Apparently the person had retired so I politely asked if someone else could sort it out. No they couldn't so I

replied "In that case the whole party will have to travel back on a normal service train without reservations." This did not go down very well at all so I enquired how else they were going to travel the 250 miles back to the Metropolis on their return ticket. Were they expected to walk? No response so I packed them all on an already full train which turned into something of a nightmare long before it got to Plymouth or Exeter.

I had more success with the Bluebell Railway who happily hired me a special train for a school outing, and many other trips on the Southern Region also went off without major mishap. The Western Region, however, was a very different matter. Although I booked 150 places on the up train to London for a large school outing one boiling hot summer's day they failed to provide any extra carriages which meant everyone, including many other disgruntled passengers, were squashed in like sardines. However, this was nothing compared to the return trip.

On arrival back at Paddington Station I was surprised to hear the station announcer say "Would Mr. Franklin please report to the Station Master's Office." I did as I was bid and was startled to be informed that a fire down the main line meant no incoming trains could get past Didcot. All they had available was a six-coach train and, as I had booked a school party, we were allowed to board first after which they would allow ordinary passengers on. The fact that these extra passengers should have been on three separate twelve-coach Bristol-bound trains meant your average sardines would have felt extremely comfortable on this particular expedition. The children, however, were delighted at the chaos.

We could not change at Swindon because there were no connecting trains available so we travelled on to Bristol Temple Meads where a diesel multiple unit was waiting for us. This was more fun for everyone and we were all in high spirits as we set off home on a different route, albeit a couple of hours late but what did that matter. We had our very own train and we were going to enjoy it. We had only travelled about 200 yards, however, before one of my colleagues, a modern railway nut, shouted "We're on the wrong line. We're going back to London!"

He was right and as the train ground to a halt the driver turned round and grinned, at which point his son did a double take as he realised it was his dad at the controls. He also realised we were on the wrong track, climbed down from the train and rang the signalman to request permission to reverse back into the station and be set on the right line. Intense excitement all round and a trip to remember.

The following year we had a diesel multiple unit to ourselves which took us all the way to London and back again. It did not travel at 100mph but the unrestricted views were great – especially for those of us who bagged the best seats behind the driver! What a great train journey, but it turned out to be the last I ever organised. Sadly, the following year there was a rail strike so we reluctantly switched to coaches, as we had already done for the annual camping trip to Cornwall after we discovered all our reserved seats on the train had been taken by other members of the public who flatly refused to move when the guard asked them.

The train had finally proved a strain too far.

LOST AT ALTON TOWERS

You may not believe this story but I swear every word of it is true! Parents and children who never have enough money for proper food, clothes or educational trips always have enough dosh for new trainers, giant TV screens and a trip to Alton Towers. Such was the case with a boy whom I shall called Wayne (not his real name but it could easily have been).

The annual trip to Alton Towers had two purposes - one for me and a few other teachers to enjoy a well-earned day out at someone else's expense, and secondly to provide enough profit to run the youth group I ran in my spare time at my own expense. So enthusiastic was I that I even persuaded my local church to fill a coach as well. Apart from a hold-up on the M5

joining the M6 at Birmingham (nothing new there then) we arrived in good time, whereupon I was promptly attacked by a very large figure dressed as Mickey Mouse who took great delight in pinching my hat and waving it in front of the pupils. Not a good start although I did, eventually, get my hat back off the human cartoon whom I could quite happily have strangled, in fact I might have attacked him back had he not been younger and bigger than me - at least I assume he was younger but I could not really tell underneath his disguise but then he was paid to have fun – at other people's expense.

I enjoyed all the rides and so did my three children. I enjoyed even more answering boys at the end of the day who said "Sir, did you go on the Corkscrew?" "Yes!" Did you enjoy the Thunderlooper?" "Yes!" In fact I went on everything!

The day passed all too quickly and soon it was time to go – well it should have been. After giving a friendly clump to a few late stragglers I told the drivers to hold on while we checked we had everyone back. We hadn't! Wayne Smith was missing. Had anyone seen him? Yes they had – an hour ago on the Pirate Ship at the far end of the park. Nothing for it but to despatch a posse and rescue him. They did and by now we were running 45 minutes late.

Off we went with me smouldering from a trip wrecked by a stupid 13-year-old with no brains and no watch – presumably no friends either because nobody had missed him. I was in the front seat of the lead coach whose driver was full of confidence about making the time up. Then we found our usual exit road closed. "Don't worry guv, I know a short cut!" Oh yeah?

After about 30 minutes I became increasingly puzzled by road signs saying "Alton Towers 19 miles" – "Alton Towers 12 miles" – "Alton Towers 8 miles." My worst fears were confirmed when the driver pulled up at a major crossroads and got out an atlas. We were lost! The next signpost said "Stoke-on-Trent 5 miles,"

We had gone round in a huge circle and were now 20 miles north of where we started off. Remember we were leading two other coaches whose younger drivers had been told to follow, and one of these coaches was full of youngsters, parents and grandparents from my church whom I had persuaded to come along for a great day out. Ouch!

Back on the M6, much further north than we should have been, I heard plaintive cries of "Can we stop for the loo, sir?" Rather than run the risk of copious amounts of smelly water running down the aisle I bowed to the inevitable and ordered a stop at Hilton Park Services ".... but only for the loo. In and out, no games – you have 5 minutes!" Five minutes came and went but not everyone was back because the only toilets in those days were situated on the northbound side (and we were heading south) so I extended it to 10 minutes. Still not everyone was back, however, so I roared into life, stormed into the games machine room, ordered everyone out and, much to the surprise of all those unconnected with my school, unceremoniously frogmarched the stragglers back.

A quick head count showed one person still missing – Wayne Smith! Oh no! I despatched the first coach home containing the church group and told the other two to wait. Armed with my trusty lieutenant we searched the entire service station, northbound and southbound, including the aforesaid games room where I heard an adult say "Cor, did you see that teacher? He wasn't half mad!" I could not stop myself from saying to him "And now I'm furious!" No sign of Wayne though! Now what?

I decided to visit the police station on the northbound side – well it was a sort of police station in a portakabin. I remember hearing myself say "You're not going to believe this but I have lost a boy". Back came the instant reply: "Would he be about 13 with mousy hair, sir?" Yes he would as I felt my anger rising and my blood beginning to boil. "He's in here playing a game of draughts and drinking a cup of cocoa. Says you left him behind, sir!" I then distinctly remember asking the policeman if he would leave the room while I murdered the wretch but what was he doing there in the first place?

A quick bit of questioning provided an unbelievable answer. Being a bear of very little brain with not even Eeyore for a friend, he had forgotten he had crossed the motorway to the toilets and searched the northbound car park before deciding he had been abandoned and told the police. They rang his mother who – as I discovered later – promptly went round to my house and harangued my wife! Good grief!

By now we were running nearly three hours late – three hours!!!!!!! But the drama had not finished yet.

The younger junior school brother of one of my other bears of very little brain – let's call him Booboo – decided it would be fun to stand up and mess about on the back seat so I decided to sit by him and keep his tired antics to a minimum. I failed because he suddenly stood up and unwittingly backed up against the emergency exit. The coach was doing 70 mph – probably more because the embarrassed driver knew it was all his fault – well not entirely. Thinking rapidly and bitterly regretting allowing younger siblings to come on the trip, I ordered the stupid little 9-year-old to sit down. "Shan't!" Visions of a fat little boy being turned into a flat little boy after being run over by a lorry as he fell from a coach, and the whole gory details being splashed across the front page of the tabloids I went for broke. In one swift movement I got up, grabbed him, sat him down and made it quite clear he was not to move a muscle until we got home. Phew!

The next drama came when we suddenly saw coach number one stranded on the hard shoulder having run out of fuel. The driver's fault again for not checking the previous driver (who was also at fault) had filled up after the last trip. Help was on the way though. Good!

We crawled in three hours late when Booboo got out and told his dad I had roughed him up. I learnt this later from another parent who overheard Booboo's dad – we'll call him Yogi – saying "Right, I'll sort him out!" This gallant Park Ranger then headed Yogi off and said if Mr. Franklin had done anything at all there would have been a very good reason, so better check it first. You will not be surprised to learn that Booboo and his older brother were later expelled. No surprise there then.

As for Wayne Smith the drama was still not over – yet! Having been banned from all future trips the following week he told me he had found a £10 note in the street. What should he do with it? "Hand it in to the local police station" was my immediate response – after all it was literally just round the corner. I knew them well – very well – so I rang and told them Master Wayne would soon be delivering a £10 note which, with any luck, would not be claimed and he could eventually keep it. His father, however, was a much bigger bear but with an even smaller brain who had apparently already decided to pocket the money.

On learning this I informed the police who went round to his house and asked for it! Mr. Bear was not a happy bunny – if you will pardon the mixed metaphor! Serve him right – and his stupid son who later played truant on school activities day but did not have enough grey cells to realise the headmaster and I would be walking straight past his house on the planned walk he had signed up for. There he was at the window – playing draughts!

LOST ON THE MALVERN HILLS

*"Let's go to the Malverns again .
The weather can't be as bad as last year."
Oh no?*

The previous year's travellers in time must have believed him because on a cold, damp, foggy morning in the middle of February a full coach load of intrepid pioneers set out to plant the school flag on the summits of both the Herefordshire and Worcestershire Beacon. Undaunted by the weather forecast our heroes started off on their first conquest but the leading group took the wrong turning almost

immediately. "Good job I brought my whistle with me" muttered the leader of the expedition as be blasted the recalcitrants back into line. "Next time you come to a junction, wait for instructions. Right?" "Right" chorused a large group of eager, beaming young faces.

One mile later came the next junction. "Which way, sir?" "To the right of course" boomed the assistant leader. "I know this section like the back of my hand" and proceeded to give a geological discourse on several invisible rocky outcrops. "Is the rock really as old as you then, sir?" said a squeaky voice whose owner narrowly avoided a thick ear.

As the mist got thicker so the visibility got shorter and some of the less trusting smaller members were heard to ask if their bigger party leaders knew exactly where we were. "Of course, you stupid boys. I've just told you I've been here before. Any moment now you will see a reservoir down on your right." "Do you mean the one down on our left, sir?" Silence! Pause for thought followed by "The map must be wrong, keep going." "But we're going the wrong way, sir!" Longer period of silence followed by a smart alec producing a compass which proved the map to be correct. Even longer pause for thought, followed by "About turn and down the steep hill to the left, we can take a short cut round the reservoir." Who was he kidding?

Cries of "Mind the bog" were heeded by everyone except John Simmons who, in his excitement not to miss his mate's latest feeble joke at the same time as doing a third take of jumping the stream for the official cameraman, forgot the old adage of "look before you leap". The result was a spectacular accident across a fallen log and a search for a missing soggy shoe in which to insert an equally soggy foot. By this time our leader had discovered the reservoir was surrounded by sharp pointed railings. After rescuing a bag thrown over by an enthusiastic member of the party intent on a kamikaze mission, it was "About turn and mind the horse muck." "Mind the what, sir?" "The horse …" Too late!

It was unanimously decided to give the Herefordshire Beacon a miss and press on to the higher summit. "Will there be any snow up there, sir?" "Of course not you stupid boy. It's much too warm." It was at this point a white, slightly wet, circular object landed in the pocket of the cameraman and rapidly melted all over his apricot fruit pie, followed immediately by a barrage of similar white-coloured objects zooming out of the fog directly into the path of the other three teachers. The leader turned round and said "Don't worry chaps, just keep your eyes straight ahead and you can dodge them as they come down the hill." "Crack" as one hit him a beauty on the back of his head before he had time to turn round again.

After dropping down from the clouds for a second time, several people thought they had finished for the day but the final push for the summit was yet to come. After clearing out every trace of food and drink from the local café it was all systems go for the Worcestershire Beacon. As the altimeter showed signs of progress, the air grew rarer and the fog grew thicker, it became increasingly difficult to identify the ghostly apparitions which melted in and out of the fog. A St. Bernard dog with a small barrel of beer and a Scottish accent turned out to be Angus Mack from the third form carrying a flask of coffee; an ugly-looking yeti turned out to be icicles hanging from the music teacher's beard; a Welsh penguin with a large rucksack turned out to be Idris Roberts the science teacher; a wailing banshee with a Yorkshire accent turned out to be the geology teacher from Barnsley singing "Land of Hope and

Glory"; and Geoffrey Smart cracking his latest feeble joke turned out to be Geoffrey Smart cracking his latest feeble joke.

If there was anything worse than the latter it was his next joke, squashed in infancy, however, by a snowball down the back of his neck. Having planted the school flag on the summit – not that anyone could see it in the fog – the party, now in good humour, set off down the hill in search of the coach which would take them home. Static poetry soon became poetry in motion interrupted only by a plaintive cry of "Sir, I'm going to be ....!" The rest I leave to your imagination but as one not very famous teacher said at the time "This is what pastoral care is all about." You can say that again ... now ... where shall we go next half term?

LOST IN LONDON

Every teacher's nightmare is losing a pupil on a school trip, the worst nightmare of all being losing a pupil in London. Here is how it happened although a couple of near misses would not go amiss first.

I once sympathised with a teacher from another school who lost a pupil in London but came dangerously close to losing a couple of mine on the Underground. The first failed to get off the train at the appointed stop and could be seen waving with a big smile on his face as the train left the station. He was no ordinary pupil and once became detached from us at Fishbourne Roman Palace. When he realised he was on the wrong side of the exhibition – you won't believe this – he ran straight across the Roman mosaic to the main party on the other side. His last primary school teacher told him he was an odds on cert to be walloped by the end of his first term at secondary school. He was right but, being something akin to the original Dennis the Menace, at an open day calmly opened the cupboard in my room, removed my pet slipper called "Horace" and stuck him on my desk with a note of explanation! How can one get cross with such genius? I came pretty close as he exited the tube station with his nose pressed against the carriage window, though, as I frantically made circular motions with my hand to suggest he got off at the next stop and return on a different train. Being a grammar school boy, even Dennis the Menace did not want to be abandoned in London and dutifully turned up ten minutes later. Phew! Exactly the same thing happened on a later trip but now I was wise to the possibility so the stupid boy knew exactly what to do as once again I frantically waved my hand in a circular motion as he disappeared into the tunnel.

Just before I changed schools I was amazed to discover a

party from my future school at the Imperial War Museum mixing with my current school so when I saw a strange boy with a red badge, went up to him and said "Watch it! I'm your new housemaster!" To say he was a bit puzzled was an understatement. The following year I took my new school to *HMS Belfast* when, sailing by on the Thames, came a boat load of pupils from my previous school. You just couldn't make it up. "Hallo sir" chorused a large group of former pupils as they sailed past on their way to Greenwich. "Can't get us now!"

All good natured of course but the real thing was not at all funny. My trips were meticulously organised and I never left anything to chance. What I did not factor in, however, was the gross negligence and stupidity of my fellow teachers. With a choice of half a dozen options in the morning, followed by everyone coming back together for lunch in Trafalgar Square, followed by another half dozen visits in the afternoon, everything in theory was foolproof. Each teacher had a colour-coded list of all their pupils and where they were going. They were also asked to check carefully they had everyone they were supposed to, before, during and after they left their particular visit. Easy! No it wasn't!

It was a hot day and everything went well – so I thought – but when one group was 30 minutes late back to the departure point on Park Lane I was cross but not alarmed. That quickly changed, however, when a teacher reported a boy missing from his coach. It still should not have been a problem, though, because he was a sensible pupil who knew he had to wait under Marble Arch if he got lost – which were in the written instructions given to every pupil before we set out. The problem was that the instructions also said we would rescue any lost soul by 5pm and it was now, thanks to the late party, 5.15! I immediately despatched the PE teacher who sprinted to Marble Arch but returned empty handed. Now what?

A quick investigation revealed the boy had been to London Zoo in the morning but had he made Trafalgar Square at lunchtime? The teacher was not sure but several boys assured me they had seen him, so had he made the trip in the afternoon? This teacher was not sure either. In fact it turned out they were all wrong! Pupils I can forgive but teachers!?

In the days before mobile phones the only option was a public phone box so we looked for the nearest one only to find it took only phone cards while the second had been vandalised. We therefore set off in convoy and stopped at the next bank of phone boxes on the Bayswater Road where I successfully dialled 999 and said "You won't believe this but I've lost a boy in London."

"Where are you sir?" "On the Bayswater Road." "OK. Wait by the kerb and we'll send a police car." I did as I was bid but 90 seconds later was astonished to hear the phone box ring from which I had just made the call. I rushed back and answered it to hear a voice say "Mr. Franklin? We've got your boy. He's at Paddington Green Police Station." How about that for service?

We quickly turned the coaches round – ever seen three coaches try to turn round on Bayswater Road? – I thought not – and headed for Paddington Green lock up which is usually reserved for high risk criminals, murderers and terrorists, where the boy was welcomed back on board. I quizzed him to discover exactly what had happened only to discover he had been left behind at London Zoo and had never been anywhere near Trafalgar Square at lunchtime. Somehow he managed to find his way to Marble Arch where he sensibly waited until 5pm then, thinking we had not missed him and left for home, approached the nearest PC Plod and explained his predicament. He was entirely blameless – apart from getting isolated in the first place – but as for the two teachers who were supposed to have been looking after him – "nil points" as they used to say in the Eurovision Song Contest but, apart from a mild rebuke, I could hardly put them in detention.

We were now on a one way system so the leading coach driver said "We'll have to go back via the North Circular, sir." Well, this turned out to be the highlight of the day because, not only had the pupils seen the sites of London such as *HMS Belfast*, Madame Tussauds, London Zoo, the RAF Museum, Trafalgar Square, River Thames, Tower of London etc. – they also saw – wait for it – Wembley Stadium! This above everything else was the biggest bonus of the day and quite outdid the saga of the missing pupil. The pupils were agog – there it was, the famous Wembley Stadium which they had only ever seen on the telly. Think of it! If only all school trips ended so happily!

PS Nowadays parents can be rather more awkward and had I not been a teacher myself, I might have been less understanding about my daughter and a younger friend getting lost in Florence on an Italian school trip organised by a very famous independent school for young ladies. The teachers took me on one side when I arrived to pick her up, explaining with very long faces what had happened. I quickly took the line she was a free spirit, as she had shown by taking charge of the other girl and making their way back by train to Sienna where they unfortunately missed the school choir singing in the "Tiger" cathedral (the Yanks christened it that during the war because of its stripy appearance). In the meantime two frantic teachers had been left behind in Florence in a fruitless search for two silly girls who had not listened to their instructions properly.

PPS It's easy to be wise after the event and I once remember telling a group of foreign students to meet me back at the minibus in London which was parked near the Post Office Tower after a day trip from Cambridge. "Remember the tower is on your left and you can't go wrong." In retrospect it was a stupid thing to say because if you think about it, wherever you are parked nearby, the tower would always be on your left if you were facing in a certain direction! Whoops. Fortunately they all found their way back and helped me put water in the radiator from a Victorian drinking fountain so we could drive home without the engine seizing up.

WAKE UP! THE SCHOOL'S ON FIRE!

For many years I led a boys residential holiday at a prep school in Devon where the headmaster became a personal friend. Stories are legion and a whole book could be written about the episodes and escapades which took place there – including how PC1 cautioned two boys who were caught pinching stuff from the local market – yes, there really was a PC1 of Devon Constabulary but the boys were actually reported to me by their mates who were appalled at what they had done. Thinking I would get little support from their parents I decided against disciplining them myself and took them straight to the police station. I was half right because when I rang one father he told me to inform his son: "He knows what to expect when he gets home!" I have never ever, before or since, seen a boy's face go pure white in less than a second. The mother of the other boy could not see what all the fuss was about, however, and clearly approved of her son's behaviour but disapproved of mine.

Sport was high on the agenda, especially annual football matches against local schools, but four other items stand out from the mass of fun related activities. Firstly. there were visits from Charles Fraser-Smith, the man who invented secret gadgets during the Second World War, the original "Q" on whom Ian Fleming modelled his own Q in the James Bond Films – played initially by Desmond Llewellyn and later by John Cleese. Secondly, there was the traditional "Hunt the Leader" when all the staff dressed up in various disguises and walked around the local town centre on market day. I was always Father Christmas and smiled inanely as the umpteenth person drawled in a broad slow West Country accent: "Bit early aren't you?" The third was a popular night wide game, a euphemism for boys being boys, camouflaging themselves in the surrounding woods while searching for treasure (bottles of pop) while being hunted by the enemy (the leaders) and being killed (their faces being liberally marked up in coloured felt tip pens) when caught. Minor accidents? Of course but nobody worried in the days before political correctness removed all elements of risk in childhood - even the boy who fell off a 10 foot high wall saw the funny side when sorted out by one of the young lady first aiders. All the boys who were caught simply glowed with excitement as they proudly showed off their felt tip "scars" – many of them, it has to be said, clever works of art - before being ordered to wash them off. "Oh sir – do we have to?" Even those who found a bottle of pop insisted on being "killed" as well.

The fourth, however, was a heart-stopping moment during which the whole world swam before my eyes. It was around 3am and I was fast asleep in the Land of Nod, dreaming of scoring the winning goal in the World Cup Final, when I was violently shaken awake by the wife of my co-leader shouting "Quick. Get up. The school's on fire!" The thoughts which raced through my head as I ran down the stairs towards the stable block - which I was informed was well ablaze – were largely along the lines of how I could inform the headmaster (who was currently on holiday in France), that we had managed to burn down his school and livelihood during his absence. The whole thing could not have taken more than a couple of minutes but it seemed like an eternity. The drama was ended, however, when the activities organiser, a local policeman as it so happened, emerged from round the block with a big smile on his face saying "Don't panic, it was only the school incinerator flaring up."

I didn't know whether to laugh or cry. Less than five minutes before, one of our young cooks had not been able to sleep and when she got up to open the window was greeted by flames shooting up behind the gym. Naturally she raised the alarm and gave us all a scare we never wished to repeat.

The corollary to this occurred the following year when, fresh from a Saturday tour match victory against the local district, our junior football team decided to celebrate by filling up three huge Victorian baths before, ignorant of both Archimedes and Samuel Plimsoll, leaping in with glee. In a normal changing room this would not have been a problem but this changing room was on the first floor with both the headmaster's study and secretary's office directly underneath. Separating them were just a few wooden floor boards and a thin covering of lino. With a desperate cry of "All hands on deck" I summoned as many leaders as I could find and, armed with mops, buckets and even a dustpan and brush we set about draining the Niagara Falls as fast as we could. We then had to agonisingly wait until Monday morning to learn if the tsunami had permeated downstairs. Amazingly, very little water seeped through the floorboards so I merely expressed surprise when told about it. Deep down, however, I was mightily relieved they never discovered the truth.

I will spare you the two occasions when D and V (diarrhoea and vomiting) swept the holiday except to say when the chips are down you soon find out who are the workers and who are the drones. Happily, there were hardly any of the latter and it gave me a quiet sense of satisfaction to see young leaders who had learned their trade as boys on earlier holidays, more than pulling their weight under pressure. Many have since gone on to positions of senior responsibility, especially within the church.

YOUR SON'S LOCKED IN A POLICE CELL

When I switched schools to the West Country from the Home Counties I encountered a type of child I had not come across before where "Yes" meant "No" and "Pardon" meant "I heard you but I wish I hadn't!" Silence meant he had heard you but was pretending he hadn't. The place I moved to was once described to me by a fellow teacher as a "A rugby league town in the south of England" and can be well illustrated by what happened in the early days of a camp in Cornwall.

I hesitated to accept a group of 15-year-olds whom I had not taught or influenced before but in the end, because money talks

if numbers are not sufficiently high, I took the risk. It proved to be a costly mistake – for them not me!

British Rail were on strike so, in absentia, hurried transport rearrangements had to be made and I hired a coach to take my group to Exeter where they would meet a similar sized group from my old school travelling by coach from London. I used to boast my ears were more like radar traps so when the grapevine began buzzing about meters being broken into in a car park during the wait for the second coach to arrive, alarm bells began to sound. The bells got louder after a couple of days when rumours reached me that a group of boys had pinched some stuff from a local shop. By now those concerned had gone lightweight camping with my co-leader on Bodmin Moor so I searched their belongings and found the stolen items as described by the shopkeeper. My mind was made up – they were going back home on the next available train (British Rail strikes notwithstanding), whatever the monetary cost to the camp.

No sooner had I made my decision than my co-leader strode into base camp the following morning with a face like thunder. Not only had the group broken camp the night before – strictly against the rules - they had also broken into a car and been apprehended by the police who were now holding them in a cell at Bodmin nick. Would I go over and sort it out. Would I? It would be a pleasure!

Three bleary eyed 15-year-olds greeted me with long faces as I strode into their cell, knowing their fate long before I spoke. They could hardly expect me to keep them on and I was certainly not going to bail them out and said so in no uncertain manner. That was their parents' job and I was just about to ring them. The phone calls, in order, went as follows:

Call Number 1: "This is Mr. Franklin calling from Cornwall to let you know your son is locked up in Bodmin Police Station for stealing." Answer: "You'd better speak to my wife."

Call Number 2: "This is Mr. Franklin calling from ..." Answer, before I had even finished speaking: "It had better be important because my wife and I are just going on holiday." I wanted to say "Perhaps you would like to make a detour via Cornwall!" but I resisted the temptation.

Call Number 3: My opening gambit resulted in the following response: "Tell him I'm getting in the car now and that he knows what to expect when I arrive around midnight!" I promised I would pass on the message which made absolutely certain the rest of his tent stayed awake to witness the anticipated fireworks. In fact it turned out to be a damp squib because by then, somewhat tired, father had calmed down a bit.

All three boys went home with their parents and none asked for a refund – just as well because I would have been extremely reluctant to part with a penny. They were later cautioned at Plymouth Police Station but, sad to say, it did not curb their kleptomaniac tendencies which resurfaced at school a short time later.

The Exeter car park theft also turned out to be true and involved at least one younger boy who was easily led but when I mentioned it to his father he replied: "Oh no. You've got it all wrong. My boy would never do a thing like that." I was sure he had but could not prove it so let the matter drop but gained no satisfaction from learning that he later served time for theft on a broader scale. How predictable. How sad!

★★★★★★★★★★★★★★★★★★★★★★★★★★

Back to the Cornwall Police who, like the Home Counties and West Country Police 35 years ago, were keen to help teachers and youth workers. Not so today where they are just as likely to prosecute them – the teachers not the children!

Llanhydrock House was the scene of a grand fete in which Cornwall Police participated and somehow managed to persuade me and my staff to take part. Dressed up in all kinds of medieval gear the chaplain ended up looking like Richard III but in charge of the horses! He had never touched one before, let alone sat on one but he did the job admirably, much to the delight of the younger members of camp. Other memories of the Police in those days are all happy ones because they were always willing to help with miscreants and always viewed young Social Services workers with justified suspicion. No longer – which is why people like me stopped running activities where unscrupulous lefties and gold diggers can cry "foul"!

I was once rung up by two young policemen who asked if I had walloped a particular truant because his mother had complained to them. I certainly had and when I said she had been into school to request it in the first place they burst out laughing. Nuff sed – after all it was not uncommon for the local police to arrest truants and then bring them straight back to school for instant justice. How times change! (see chapter on how I broke a shoplifting syndicate while the Queen was in town).

Devon Police also joined in the fun during Hunt the Leader when I dressed up as Father Christmas and other leaders were resplendent in drag and all kinds of splendid disguise although the chaplain once got arrested in Cornwall for dressing up as a bank robber complete with stocking mask and plastic machine gun. He had been reported by a new non-Cornish shopkeeper who was instantly ostracised by the local traders whom we knew well and enjoyed our annual visits. The chaplain, however, never used the disguise again.

Back in the West Country I was once rung up and asked if I could identify a boy who had attacked an old lady, simply by his description. Piece of cake! I knew at once who had done it. His criminal family later pinched our school minibus during the summer holidays, brazenly took it to Alton Towers, nicked some petrol without paying en route, then returned it – damaged! Luckily, by then I had spotted it missing and had informed the police.

On another occasion the Police needed to identify some young shoplifters so I was invited by the store detective to view the CCTV film at a well-known large department store. No problem at all but the one thing which connected all these petty miscreants was the absence of a father figure at home. Nuff sed – except that more than once I was begged for help by a single mother at her wit's end! How sad.

SHOPLIFTING AND THE QUEEN

Before the Queen visited the town to open a new school I jokingly said to my wife "It'll be a shoplifters' paradise." When she asked what I meant I laughingly explained how easy it would be for thieves to nip in the shops while the assistants watched the regal procession. How right I was but not in the way I expected it.

Everything began to unravel a few days later when, as Head of Lower School, I received a police notification of a caution administered for shoplifting to a thoroughly respectable 12-year-old boy whom I knew well from church and youth group.

EXCUSE ME SIR BUT WE'VE HAD A CALL FROM A TEACHER SAYING HE'S CAUGHT A DOZEN LADS SHOPLIFTING WHILE THE QUEEN WAS IN TOWN!!

As was my custom, I called him in and asked how on earth someone like him could have been so stupid. I shall never forget his reply: "It wasn't just me, sir. I was the only one who got caught!" Having ascertained he had been thrashed by his father I asked him to elaborate.

Like me, he and plenty of others had thought of the easy pickings while the Queen went by. So easy had it proved that they had widened their shoplifting syndicate into quite an operation. Fagin had nothing on this lot. I contacted the police, told them of my suspicions and was invited to investigate further at school but to keep them in the loop. It was not long before more than a dozen Artful Dodgers willingly confessed, with stolen property rolling in by the day. I contacted the police

again who told me as I was making far better progress than they were, would I please take over the entire investigation and let them know when I had finished. We had already agreed that, owing to the potential numbers involved and with full parental approval, I would discipline every one at school and they would administer an official caution. Simple, easy and the slate would be wiped clean for all.

Within a fortnight, however, my office resembled an Aladdin's cave with every kind of stolen merchandise you can imagine. Even the supposedly foolproof system of long playing records being checked through an electronic turnstile at WH Smith's had been ingeniously and successfully by-passed. The culprits were, perhaps surprisingly or perhaps not, mainly middle class or bright working class kids aged 12-13 and I received full parental support from every single one. Punishment was meted out according to how much had been taken, on the strict understanding that all contraband had to be handed in. One bright spark tried to beat the system, however, but was promptly shopped by his chums-in-crime and received a double whammy for his subterfuge.

Then came the first of two unusual twists. Firstly, one of the boys also admitted to stealing hundreds of Royal Mail items from letterboxes as he did his paper round over a period of several months. The whole lot was stashed under his bed! "Please sir, what am I going to do?" This was a far more serious crime and one which I anticipated would land him in court so both the police and I put him on the back burner.

The second twist was even more bizarre. When informed that Stephen (not his real name), one of my star footballers and a quiet, very polite boy but with an extremely tough father, had stolen stamps from the main post office, my heart sank. I rang his dad thinking he would veto any idea of school punishment and administer his own form of justice. I was therefore astonished to hear him say: "Right! I'm coming down to school this minute and I'm going to watch you deal with him!" I couldn't believe my ears but he was true to his word. I collected the boy from class to gasps of amazement – they had correctly surmised my sudden appearance – and brought him face to face with his apoplectic father. I felt genuinely sorry for the tearful lad as his dad shouted "Take it son!" but am certain he was relieved to have been caught, punished and forgiven. It was also much better he had been dealt with dispassionately at school rather than at home.

The police were delighted with the turn of events. Something approaching 20 boys had been caught shoplifting; every one had been disciplined with full parental approval; everyone had been cautioned; most of the stolen property had been returned intact to its owners and the school grapevine knew that shoplifting was off limits, at least for the time being.

The newspaper boy was – very generously in my opinion – given a caution instead of a court appearance and his mightly relieved parents were more than happy for me to sort him out at school. In fact they sent me a letter of thanks after it was all over. Even the boy himself expressed his appreciation at what he saw as being let off the hook. Imagine all this happening today!

I would be surprised if more than a couple of the junior Fagins ever re-offended and personally regret that physical justice coupled with instant forgiveness is now a thing of the past.

WADING ACROSS THE ESTUARY

Camping is great! I met my wife on a camp and all three of my children benefited too, eventually as junior leaders. Little did I ever imagine, however, that the first camp I attended in Cornwall as a 15 year old would influence the rest of my life in a dramatic manner. In pre-motorway days it took two days to get there from Manchester and when our minibus crested the hill near the end of the journey it quite took my breath away. Used to dull grey seas on the Lancashire coast here was a brilliant blue expanse of water shimmering under a hot sun with a glowing azure sky in between. Add to that the rugged green-topped cliffs and I was instantly hooked. Only those who have been to Cornwall will understand the special light which attracts artists by the bucket load.

"I've never recorded the music for a David Attenborough film before!"

Within a matter of a few years I graduated through the ranks and became leader of the camp for nearly 20 years during which time many good things happened and a large number of boys went on to become full time Christian workers and ministers. It therefore seems incongruous to flag up some things which went wrong but mishaps are always more interesting.

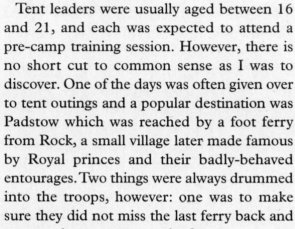

Tent leaders were usually aged between 16 and 21, and each was expected to attend a pre-camp training session. However, there is no short cut to common sense as I was to discover. One of the days was often given over to tent outings and a popular destination was Padstow which was reached by a foot ferry from Rock, a small village later made famous by Royal princes and their badly-behaved entourages. Two things were always drummed into the troops, however: one was to make sure they did not miss the last ferry back and the second to keep enough money to pay the fare.

One hot day everyone returned on time apart from a tent of stragglers who rolled in half an hour after tea. They were all soaked to the skin, including their leader, so I naturally enquired what on earth they had been up to. His reply temporarily rendered me speechless. "We got stranded at Padstow without any money so we walked back across the sand." After I recovered my composure I asked "But what about the water in the middle?" "Oh, it came up to our necks but we were OK!" My flabber was well and truly gasted as I told him he had just led his boys across the tidal estuary of the River Camel, an extremely dangerous stretch of water at the best of times. All I can imagine is that he, a supposedly intelligent grammar school boy, and his tent of boys must have waded across as the tide was turning otherwise they would all have been swept upstream or out to sea. Phew!

Another potential catastrophe was set in motion by a naive staff officer who, strictly against the rules, allowed an unaccompanied group of boys out after dark. When they did not return for the evening meeting alarm bells began to sound and I quickly organised a search party. A wide beach with a surging incoming tide in the pitch dark was not an easy place to explore, nor were the sheer cliffs on either side. Everyone's child is precious but amongst the party was my church pastor's son who, as it subsequently turned out, was instrumental in their prank as he organised their concealment as they watched their worried leaders searching for them. I doubt he ever told his dad and I certainly didn't.

No children were allowed in the sea without proper adult supervision but this did not apply to the catering staff. While the chaplain and I were strolling along the beach one afternoon we spotted one of our young lady cooks dashing in for a dip and, both being very experienced with the local tides, immediately realised that where she had left her clothes would in less than five minutes, be completely submerged. We hurriedly moved them further up the beach and waited. About 15 minutes later the young lady emerged from the surf only to discover her mistake. We let her look frantically for a couple of minutes and think everything had been swept out to sea before emerging with the said garments safe and sound. After that I made sure that no single adults were to bathe alone.

It is a sad fact of life that most boys are tempted to pinch things. I did it myself once and, although I was not the actual guilty party, I happily shielded the thief in Woolworth's and was more than happy to share the proceeds of a Cadbury's Snack right underneath the statue of Sir Robert Peel who founded the Police force. I believe we even jokingly offered him a piece.

In dealing with miscreants I always took into account the nature of the beast and what he took (girls rarely steal until they are older). One silly boy, an asthmatic, pinched some sweets on an outing and, as soon as he found out someone had snitched on him but before I got to hear about it, simply legged it. The fact he was miles from home in a strange county did not occur to him and quite where he thought he was going I have no idea. To this day I am grateful to the person who discovered him hiding in their garden shed and returned him in their car to camp to face the music. They never stopped to give their name so, if you are reading this some 35 years later, may I offer you my heartfelt thanks. His parents were duly shocked and, apart from returning the stolen goods – or what was left of them – no further action was needed on my part.

Only once in my career did I fail to respond to a medical matter and I made sure it was my last. I was woken on camp at 2am by a senior staff officer who told me one of his junior leaders, a sensible 16 year old, had stomach pains. I am not at my best at that hour so simply asked if he had checked for an appendicitis. He had – or so he told me. An hour later he woke me again. Things had got worse so I went to investigate. It was immediately obvious the lad was in great distress and a gentle poke in the right place told me he had an acute appendicitis. In the days before mobile phones it was a case of find the nearest phone box which was in the local village where I rang the operator and asked if I could speak to a duty doctor.

I explained the symptoms and my diagnosis to which he replied "Are you sure you know what you are talking about?" I assured him I did to which he responded with "Your best bet is to get him to hospital as fast as you can. An ambulance will take too long and you have a choice of Plymouth or Truro." The latter, although nearly 40 miles away, was slightly nearer and is the only hospital open at night in the whole of Cornwall.

I commandeered another leader as back up, gently put the patient in the back of my car and raced off into the night. Dawn was breaking as we arrived at Treliske Hospital where I was mightily miffed when, after my explanation, the clerk on duty said haughtily "We make the diagnosis not you." Needless to say, I was right and the lad was sliced shortly afterwards. When his grateful parents came down from Surrey to pick him up they made a considerable detour to offer their personal thanks.

Never again did I fail to check a child who complained of feeling ill – which is why I was extremely angry when I once discovered a boy had been put in the school medical room without my knowledge and totally without supervision. By the time I found out and went to investigate he had literally kicked a hole in the wall because he was in so much pain (see Chapter 6). Another candidate for a hasty scalpel.

Back to camp …….. there are so many stories to tell, especially about gales bringing down marquees and tents in the middle of the night – not to mention the years when D & V (diarrhoea and vomit) ravaged both the camp and surrounding district when, with just one tap to serve 100 people, it would have been impossible to survive without everyone pulling together in the most remarkable manner.

Three frivolous stories spring to mind. During a night wide game, a leader and a boy tangled on a hillside and in rolling down the hill went head first straight through a large fresh cow pat. Yuk! The cooks took pity on them both and liberally sprayed them from a distance with the hosepipe before eventually washing their hair.

Driving the school minibus back from a day out to the Scilly Isles I found it difficult to keep up with the cars in front so three days later was mightily dischuffed to receive in the post a summons for speeding on the St. Austell bypass. I could not deny it and the school name was on the side of the vehicle but how had they managed to trace me to a local camp site so quickly? Retreating to my tent in a depressed state I occupied myself in paperwork but was awoken from my depression by what sounded like the whole camp chanting my name. I emerged to discover everyone sitting under the camp flag with huge grins on their faces. Behind them was my camp organiser waving what looked like a suspicious carbon copy of an official document. It was! He had set me up with the connivance of his mates in the Devon and Cornwall Constabulary who had issued a summons in the sure knowledge I would exceed the speed limit on this particular stretch of dual carriageway. Now I understood why he had accelerated so quickly in front of me, thus forcing me to go faster than normal. Later in the camp he burst a tyre by colliding with a rock jutting out on a narrow country lane and I later got a police inspector friend to set him up for speeding on the M5. Unfortunately, he rumbled it but told the inspector "If you'd chosen the M4 instead of the M5 then I would have believed you!"

North Cornwall is full of hidden coves and we often had one to ourselves. The path down was very steep, though, so it was my practice to go on ahead and supervise. On one particular occasion, however, my co-leader and I did a double take as we crested the cliff top because there below us were three stark naked young ladies having the time of their lives lolloping in the surf. We hurried down, discussing en route how we could avoid a situation which every boy would relate with glee to his parents once he got home. The trio turned out to be rather attractive German frauleins in their early-twenties so my chum, a bachelor, volunteered to explain how, at any moment, the whooping cavalry would come charging over the hilltop so perhaps they might like to consider putting back on some of the stitches they had completely removed. They did, although not many of them.

The final incident was one for the Keystone Cops. The same co-leader and I were all alone in the local cafe when in came a grandmother, daughter and granddaughter. Amazingly, although they had the whole café to chose from, they squashed up tightly behind my friend which forced him up against the table. He responded by wriggling violently which pushed the grandmother's large umbrella into her back. This went on for about 30  seconds before there was a volcanic explosion caused by the erupting grandmother who literally attacked him. A heavy glass ashtray smashed to smithereens on the floor before the manager hurriedly emerged to evict everyone! Happily, a couple of boys from another camp had just arrived, witnessed the whole event and spoke up for us. Before we left, my chum generously paid for both sets of food and drink, so our good reputation remained intact. That evening at camp, I received a visit from the mother demanding to speak to my friend but in my best deputy headmastorial manner I defused the situation and thus avoided a second confrontation.

Camp was fun and, just like me, I believe many found it a life changing experience. How sad that young people today rarely experience such a holiday. Two true stories make my final point.

When I agreed to take 13-year-old Clint his housemaster told me I was mad – so did the headmaster. I went ahead anyway and when I got back they were keen to know how he got on. My answer was concise: "He never put a foot wrong!" They didn't believe me at first until I explained how, for the first time in his life, he had been surrounded by caring adults who took a genuine interest in him. Sadly, he later became a one man crime wave and spent more time in prison than out.

I never found out what happened to Jeremy but after he had bullied a younger boy on camp I gave him a dose of his own medicine with the words: " Now you know what it feels like!" He was profoundly apologetic both to me and to his victim but, as I later discovered, it clearly went much deeper. When we got home he was the last person I dropped off from the school minibus but as he climbed out he turned to me and said words I shall never forget: "Sir – I want to thank you for the most fantastic holiday I have ever had in my life …….. but I think you ought to know I'm in court tomorrow for GBH!"

ALBERT GOES TO CAMP

You've heard of young Albert Ramsbottom.
Who was eaten by lion in't zoo,
How he came back again from his stomach
As good if not better than new.

The experience frightened young Albert
For lions are always unkind,
But when he first went off to Cornwall
It scared him clean out of his mind.

He ventured to try it one summer
As he'd heard of this wonderful camp,
So he put on his best jeans and T-shirt
Which made him look just like a tramp.

He was greeted upon his arrival
By dozens of lads, clean and neat,
Who sat on his head and his stomach
And frog marched him in for a treat.

He was thrust in a tent with some urchins
Who demolished it into wreck,
And after they went into breakfast
Poured green porridge down Albert's neck.

Poor Albert had hardly recovered
His breath when they started to eat,
He didn't like porridge but cornflakes
So they left him glued to his seat.

Albert wouldn't get up the next morning,
His tent leader's face was a blank
But the boys in his tent were less thoughtful
And dunked him head first in the tank.

The wide games astonished our hero
Who was weak and lacking in trust,
When told to climb through some barbed wire
Young Albert, poor lad, did his crust.

At football our hero was hopeless.
T'was a mountain he just couldn't climb,
Till he thought he'd scored his first goal
Then realised they'd changed round at half time.

For nearly two week the camp lasted,
He can't make no sense of it still
But when't teacher said "Come next year Albert?"
He answered "I certainly will!"

A LIFE ON THE OCEAN WAVE

School trips abroad included French excursions to Normandy and four days in Tunisia on a Freddie Laker inspired Aerocruise field trip. Unfortunately, Laker Airways went bust before the scheme really got going, but I was amused to discover the headmaster of a large comprehensive school who joined me as the company adviser had told his secretary he was on a conference in Oxford! It was a good trip although I had a brief nightmare when I realised we had stumbled into the red light district of Sousse in Tunisia. It took me only a second to realise they were not horses behind the stable doors but painted ladies of all ages, shapes and sizes in what was obviously the public brothel. Yikes! I hastily did an about turn and ordered my pupils to do the same. To this day I am not sure if they understood why but happily they were not present when my colleague and I were approached in the street later that evening asking if we needed a prostitute, any age or sex could be supplied without problem. We politely declined.

However, it was seven educational cruises which must take pride of place – six on *ss Uganda* and one on the smaller ill-fated *ms Jupiter*. They were wonderful experiences with the magic of being on board ship in the middle of an empty sea when the world might be consumed by nuclear war and you would not realise it, so calm and still was the setting. This was especially true at night when one could be outside on deck in the dark all alone, save for the lapping of the waves as the boat ploughed on almost silently into the night.

I counted it a privilege to have organised all but the first one myself, choosing the itineraries and giving the kids a really beneficial educational experience. It was fascinating to visit both Israel and Egypt where the inhabitants of each asked us what the other was like because they had never been there. We failed to visit Jerusalem at the first attempt because of bombing, likewise Cyprus. Instead we visited Lebanon, ironically just before the civil war began, and Rhodes respectively. I actually kept Lebanon a secret from both the pupils and their parents, although one dad, an airline pilot, asked me to surreptitiously let him know because he was going to be away and thought we might meet up! Incredible that nobody thought this unusual at

the time. Imagine allowing your children to go on a foreign holiday today not knowing which countries they would be visiting!

What were the highlights? Madeira was a fantastic island but has since been riddled with EU-funded motorways while the Pyramids turned out to be situated on the outskirts of Cairo. The Garden Tomb in Jerusalem was spiritually uplifting, which is more than can be said for the more commercial sights, while Capernaum, Nazareth, the Sea of Galilee and the Dead Sea were memorable for different reasons. One could float in the latter but had to be very careful not to get salt in the eyes, while the Sea of Galilee provided me with a unique opportunity to film waves crashing over the boat reacting to the afternoon choppy weather, just like the story of Jesus in the Bible. I placed a copy of *The Living Bible* on deck and started to roll the camera. When I had finished the young female Israeli guide asked me what the book was. When I explained she came out with the classic statement: "But we only have the Shakespeare version!" I later posted her a copy of a modern translation!

It was on the island of Malta that I nearly met my Waterloo when I leant against the back of a coach window to film the coach following behind. The next thing I knew I was hanging out of an empty frame trying to keep my balance as the rear windscreen disappeared from view under the front wheels of the following vehicle. Having managed to pull myself back in I tried to explain my predicament to the driver who merely shrugged his shoulders as if nothing had happened. When we arrived at our destination, the old city of Medina high on the hill in the centre of the island, I was amazed when a short time later my co-leader emerged from the other bus with a big grin on his face, carrying a complete rear windscreen with a huge tyre mark right across the middle. It was plastic and clearly they were used to losing it!

I enjoyed being the geologist on a single boat load of experts who trod the crater of an active volcanic island in the middle of the Santorini caldera, broadcasting back over the circling ship's tannoy as the captain singed his bottom by venturing too close to the centre! It was good to stand on Mars Hill on the Areopagus where Paul preached in Athens and to visit the sites of six of the Seven Ancient Wonders of the World, the only exception being the Hanging Gardens of Babylon in Iraq, although all the others are in various states of disrepair or disappearance. The ruined city of Ephesus was brilliant and Venice memorable for perhaps the wrong reasons - smells and dogs' mess! Greek islands have a charm of their own but then so did everywhere else we went. I also made sure we got the best value for money by choosing fly-cruises out of Gatwick although the last of all was an experience I never wish to repeat.

It was October 16th, 1987 and I thought something was odd as we drove along the M25 in the dark because the coach kept veering from side to side. Most of the pupils were asleep when the driver stopped and asked if I would help him get the windscreen wipers going again. As I stepped outside I noticed the grass was horizontal and there was a very strong wind blowing. It got worse!

We arrived at Gatwick at 3.30am and checked into the departure lounge, being almost the only party there. I noticed the huge windows, about 15 feet high, were bowing in the wind and went to investigate the weather outside. Then it happened .... with a terrific crash, two of the enormous panes of glass blew in, fell straight down the stairwell in front of me and shattered. Had they not been several inches thick and incredibly heavy then I would have been shredded to pieces. A couple of security guards rushed in with ashen faces and gasped: "Is there anyone down there?" When I told them I was the only person in the vicinity they heaved a huge sigh of relief.

More windows then collapsed by which time the airport was in total chaos.

The night before, BBC Weatherman, Michael Fish had infamously said there was no danger of a gale but it totally devastated south east England and toppled hundreds of thousands of trees. I managed to phone home and was relieved to hear the gale had not touched down there but the poor man behind me in the queue, like hundreds of others, had just lost the roof off his house. We were eventually evacuated from the departure lounge back into the main concourse by which time it was overflowing, all flights having been cancelled either a) because it was not safe to take off; b) not safe to land; or c) the aircraft was stranded somewhere else. I was on my own with a dozen children, no information, nowhere to sit and nothing to do. "When are we going, sir?" became the stuff of nightmares.

It turned out that all trains had been suspended because of fallen trees across the tracks and many expectant passengers literally walked along the railway lines to Gatwick! Our cruise headquarters was at nearby Haywards Heath but nobody could get in or out. Later that evening a loudspeaker call came for school party leaders to assemble when I discovered someone I knew vaguely from my camping past had taken control of the situation. To cut a long story short they eventually found us a plane around midnight and we arrived in Athens at about 3am. We missed our trip to the Acropolis but had a fantastically clear night-time view of the city as we came in to land after circling round from the sea.

Exactly 12 months after this cruise, the same ship, *ms Jupiter* was in collision with a freighter just outside Piraeus harbour and sank with the loss of four lives. The friend who took control at Gatwick gave me a full account of what happened and of the bravery of a sixth form pupil who used his body as a bridge for people to walk across to safety as the ship went down.

Did the children benefit in any way from these school cruises? Not 'arf! After three days at sea including the Bay of Biscay, the first port of call on the very first cruise was the island of Madeira which we approached as dawn broke. What a fantastic sight as the steeply shelving volcanic island loomed up out of the early morning mist. Once ashore we were ushered onto a very modern coach and when I asked the driver where it was built I was amazed to discover it was British. High up in the mountains along winding narrow roads we came across barefooted children which was quite a surprise. Down on the beach at Camara de Lobos, where Winston Churchill once painted, we came across a load of happy naked urchins whose day was apparently spent running in and out of the sea. It was an eye opener for my largely wealthy pupils and reminded me of what the Victorian period must have been like. I was told by later visitors that Madeira is now criss-crossed by tunnels paid for with so called European Union money which is a complete misnomer. I think I prefer Madeira as it was with innocent happy children just being innocent happy children. For those who don't understand this comment then I recommend Neil Postman's excellent book *The Disappearance of Childhood*.

When we stopped at Casablanca we all expected to see a bit of North Africa but all the guides wanted to show us was a Roman Catholic cathedral. Across the Mediterranean at Malaga was even worse because after enduring a three hour bus journey to Granada we were given a long boring trip around the Alhambra Palace, enlivened only by police chasing some gypsies up and down the street. Next time, when I was in charge, it would be different – and it was! I made sure we saw the countries we were visiting and, more importantly, the people who lived in them. Churches were replaced by street markets and camel rides – much more interesting than dusty ruins.

Actually, not all ruins were a disaster and a couple of enlightened guides brought the Roman Empire to life by showing us the ruts made by chariot wheels, and channels where refuse was thrown from the shops at the end of daily trading. The highlight though was undoubtedly the communal toilets at Ephesus where everyone had to have their photograph taken sitting next to each other on the well preserved stone toilet seats.

I made certain the pupils got the best of everything in Israel and Egypt (although I had to remonstrate with a camel owner who tried to hijack one of my charges at the Pyramids), Lebanon, Rhodes, Athens, Venice and all stations hundreds of miles south of Paddington. At Olympia I picked up a few of the thousands of tiny fossils which had dropped from the ruined Temple of Zeus but when a guide spotted one of my pupils doing the same he went bananas. I ushered the boy away and once round the corner gave him a few of mine.

When we landed at Malta there was a spontaneous burst of applause from 300 nervous children who obviously thought their last moment had arrived. Only one did not join in because he was busy trying to wipe the sick off his school blazer. I never personally suffered from travel sickness but I did puke up just once during a cruise, not because I was seasick but because all the children in the dormitory were retching during a storm and the dormitory floor must have been two inches deep in vomit. I had gone down to help but soon beat a hasty retreat to the nearest loo before I was completely trapped. Meantime the Indian stewards calmly swept everything up with a dustpan and brush and emptied it into a large plastic dustbin. It was obviously happening all over the ship and they were clearly immune. Before I fled I was amused to see a matron whip the vomit soaked pyjamas from the same boy who puked up on the plane leaving him somewhat bemused. All I could say before I fled upstairs to puke myself was "Wear a T-shirt and shorts".

I actually enjoy a good blow at sea but one morning I awoke to find my feet were higher than my head. The next moment the situation was reversed and I quickly realised we were in a force 10 gale. Dressing hurriedly I went up on deck to see a dark grey Adriatic Sea heaving with indignation and the ship bobbing up and down like a cork as we staggered past Albania. There was nobody else around and only six out of 60 teachers turned up for breakfast. The troops down below fared little better but were proud to inform their parents they had survived a hurricane – well not quite but it was an experience not to be forgotten.

John Drinkwater was aptly named. We have all seen amusing pictures from *You've Been Framed* where a hapless individual topples over into something nasty. In John's case it was the camera trick in reverse. The location was Gythion in Greece, a small port where the ship anchored offshore and we all transferred by lifeboat to the quayside. I never believed in wrapping children up in cotton wool so allowed my troops to go around in groups of not less than three. After all what could possibly go wrong in a small fishing village? Plenty!

John was taking a picture of his group when he realised they would not quite fit into the frame of his lens but instead of asking them to move back, he retreated. Still they were not quite in shot so he retreated a little further. Those present insisted Laurel and Hardy could not have done it better as he achieved a backward somersault with pike and twist straight into the harbour – in his school uniform. Fortunately, he could swim and, after paddling to the nearby steps, persuaded one of the lifeboats to take him back on board for a change of clothing. I arrived on the scene just too late to enjoy the fun.

Most countries spoke some English but Dubrovnik in the former Yugoslavia was the exception. Only by pointing to an item could a purchase be made but when my colleague and I decided to buy 72 small pots of honey to give as a present to each of our troops to take home to their families we met our Waterloo, Victoria, Euston and Kings Cross all combined. No amount of buzzing noises or flapping our arms did any good so we settled for 72 pots of jam instead. On a second visit to the same shop on a later cruise I fared even worse. Having just purchased a bottle of red wine which was handed to me in a flimsy plastic bag I gently put it down on the stone floor – at least I thought I had but the bottle turned out to be as flimsy as the carrier bag. Having heard a gentle chink I picked it back up to see if anything had happened. While I was pondering why the glass had apparently frosted over it completely disintegrated and I was left holding just the neck. The rest of the plonk and a million tiny fragments of glass were now distributed all over the floor. I have never seen my colleague move so fast as he fled through the door leaving me, as red as the former wine in the bottle, to face the music. Not a word was said, however, as a cleaner silently emerged from the back with a dustpan and brush and swept up the mess. I discreetly apologised – in English – bought another bottle and also fled the scene as fast as I could.

A different colleague had a very nasty scare in Jerusalem. While I was busy trying to buy a fake fur hat from a street trader, he disappeared round the corner shouting at the troops to keep up. I borrowed one of them, told him which hat I wanted and got him to surreptitiously buy it at a much cheaper price than the vendor would have sold it to me. We then chased after the rest of the party only to find an ashen faced teacher quaking in his boots. "You'll never guess what I've just done!" was all he could stutter. I couldn't so he told me. "I've only just walked straight through Cyrus Vance's armed bodyguard and bumped straight into him!" It transpired he had been walking backwards shouting at the pupils and did not see the armed group coming towards him. After accidentally jostling the US Secretary of State who was there on his umpteenth peace mission, he was promptly and unceremoniously picked up and thrown to one side amidst a flurry of machine guns. Whoops! No wonder his face was as white as a sheet.

Bodrum in Turkey was the scene of a battle between The Crusaders and Islamists with cannon ball damage clearly visible in the ancient walls. It was also the site of one of the Seven Wonders of the Ancient World, the Tomb of Halicarnassus. Surprisingly, unlike the other six, this is the very last place they want you to see but, undaunted, my colleague and I felt we ought at least to take a peek at what was left of it. The official guides would have none of it so we paid a couple of locals to take us through the back streets to find a total wreck, stripped of all its former glory in order to build the later town. The same thing happened to the Pyramids at Cairo where the alabaster coverings of all three were removed to help build the modern city next door. Now you know why the Great Pyramid of Giza looks as though it is snow capped –because the alabaster at that height was too difficult to remove!

Seven educational cruises was a privilege. I took every one very seriously and made certain my pupils got only the very best because, on the six I was in charge of, I made absolutely certain they saw local poverty alongside the tourist attractions. They were trips of a lifetime and I know they were appreciated by children and parents alike.

What a pity that cruises of this kind no longer take place.

WHO STOLE MY FOOTBALL BOOTS?

Down the years I carefully nurtured good relations with several prep schools in respect of junior football fixtures. It was good for both sets of boys to mix and see how things were done differently. Much was learned by both sides and I remember one amusing incident where the showers were being supervised by a young looking matron (not unusual in a prep school) but at which two of my more developed 12 year olds protested. My response was immediate: "Hard luck mate – in you go while she's not looking!"

I always gave secret instructions not to win by more than one goal and if at all possible to manufacture a score draw which

SORRY ABOUT THIS MRS YATES - BUT AS YOU CAN SEE - WE'RE STILL DESPERATELY SHORT OF A LOLLIPOP CROSSING PERSON!

STOP

AAGHH!!

kept everyone happy and the fixture willingly renewed the following season. I came unstuck with one school, however, because every member of their all-conquering team of the year before had left but nobody had thought to tell me so I selected a team which was much too strong and, despite dire warnings whispered from the touchline to ease off, scored nine goals. Ouch! I apologised afterwards to their teacher who had already given his boys a right rollicking and to the headmaster who was extremely gracious. During the match itself, however, I got chatting to an elegantly dressed man with a smart cloth cap and all the trappings of a cultured country gent, to whom I took an instant liking. His face seemed vaguely familiar but it was not until after the match that I realised who he reminded me of - the former Home Secretary, Robert Carr. I mentioned it to their teacher who replied" "Yes! That was Lord Carr watching his grandson!" What a nice man. Happily, this was not the school to which the rest of this story is devoted.

I have never suffered fools gladly and certainly not small ones with no brains. One brainless idiot in particular raised my hackles so much that I felt it necessary to ask their teacher to stand by me in case I murdered the wretch. To my shame it was the one and only time I ever swore at a pupil – albeit in the mildest possible manner. The scenario took place as follows and I promise you it is true although you probably won't believe it!

Prep school matches often took place on Wednesday afternoons and were always played away – which was half the fun as the games were followed by high tea which my pupils loved. I only ever took boys whom I could trust and on this particular occasion banned a boy who had caused trouble the previous weekend. He simply could not be trusted – how right I was! Wednesday afternoon arrived and because both minibuses were already booked I asked for parental cars instead. No problem and we duly turned up, played the two matches and started eating tea – which is when things began to unravel, quickly, much too quickly and finally at an alarming rate.

Their teacher was a friend but when he approached me with the words "I don't want to cause a fuss but ..." I knew something was wrong. One of his team's spare pair of football boots had disappeared from the touchline and he had been informed that one of my boys had taken them. I could not believe my ears and said I could hardly credit it but would investigate immediately. Big-eared Jimmy Smith, who had been hovering nearby, clearly knew what had happened, though, and was dying to tell me. "It was Clint Jones, sir!" Again, I could not believe my ears and heard myself saying "But he's not here, I banned him." "Oh yes he is, sir. He stowed away in Mr. Booth's car and watched from the touchline where you couldn't see him!" Shock horror and pause for sharp intake of breath. Could this be true? Not only did we have a stowaway but a thief to compound the situation.

My blood was beginning to boil. "Where is he now?" "Outside, sir. Shall me and the boys fetch him?" I agreed without realising the consequences but it was not long before I found out. About five minutes later an ashen-faced matron staggered in from her upstairs sitting room and gasped "I've just seen several boys chasing another boy in and out of the cars down the main road!" This was going from bad to worse. Another five minutes elapsed which seemed more like five years in which I scarcely knew what to say. All the work I had carefully built up over so many years was in danger of going down the tubes in one appalling incident which, for all I knew, had already resulted in at least one pupil knocked over on a busy main road. It was therefore with a mixture of relief, despair and anger when I saw the aforesaid Clint Jones frog-marched in by a bunch of smiling team mates who looked just like a pack of wolves who had just made their first kill. Big-eared Jimmy spoke up for the successful posse:' "'Ere you are sir, we had a bit of trouble but we finally caught 'im 'alf a mile down the road!" I imagined it was more like 'in the road' but never mind, the quarry had been well and truly cornered.

At this point I asked their teacher to come with me as I took the wretch outside and gave him a real verbal ear-bashing. I was aghast that someone could do something so underhand. I was known to be firm but was always regarded as fair, a phrase which came not from me but from a parent (see chapter on Alton Towers) but this was a really low shot. It was water off a duck's back, however, and I have little doubt the brainless oaf later transgressed the law at a higher level. My headmaster was no help at all when I explained what had taken place which is why the staff and parents always came to me when there was a problem.

Happily, their teacher was extremely gracious and, as I already knew the headmaster from a previous school, all was smoothed over and forgiven. On a later visit with a different age group from a different school, I entered the changing rooms after the match was over to find an agitated and very wet 9 year old who had just stepped out of the shower protesting vigorously that someone had stolen his clothes. I responded with "Did you remember to transfer them when we switched changing rooms just before the match began?" Errrrrrrrrr!

SIR! THERE'S A GIRL IN OUR SHOWER!

Would I lead a sporting exchange to our twin town in France? I certainly would but on condition I took other experienced teachers with me. Agreed.

The Under 14 district school football team was duly assembled (I was both Secretary and Chairman of the Association) but there was nobody to take charge of the Under 12 rugby team which was hastily put together from my own school at the last minute. In the absence of any rugby teachers guess who was asked to run it? My experience of rugby union was always coloured by my love of rugby league and to this day I still cannot understand all the rules – neither, it seems, can many TV pundits!

Our early exit from Calais was in the small hours and just about everyone was asleep – apart from me. Then it happened - two French cars came hurtling across the top of a grassy roundabout and just missed our coach. It took me a couple of seconds to realise why. Our driver – perhaps he was half asleep as well - had forgotten we were in France and had driven the wrong way round the roundabout. No wonder the frog machines scattered in all directions!

We eventually arrived safe and sound and the younger troops and I were billeted in a run-down hostel on the edge of the large provincial town. No problem as we were entirely separate on the top floor, well away from the noisy goings on lower down. A strange incident occurred when the allocation of older pupils to French homes took place, however, because when our star centre forward (striker in modern parlance) was called out, the French organiser hastily said there had been a mistake and called out the next name. It transpired the host was a racist and our delightful player was non-white (how I hate the expression "black"). Just to show how it never affected the pupils in my school, while on a residential trip to Devon we organised a "back-to-front" meal where everything was done in reverse. The other six boys in his dormitory blacked their features while he whited his. Terrific!

The junior rugby match went well and we won, albeit narrowly, but the French were aghast. They had not played well so could they have a rematch? I thought this was ridiculous but not wanting to offend our hosts I agreed and we duly beat them again. During the second game one of my team was trampled to the ground by a very large Frog. "Get up!" I shouted. "Can't" snivelled the wretch. "Yes you can" I replied as I poured half a bucket of cold water over him. It did the trick and the game was resumed.

Now to the changing rooms where we handed out beautiful glass mugs with an engraved town crest to all our hosts. Within 60 seconds two of them had been dropped and smashed to smithereens. Had we got any more? Yes we had but I was blowed if I was going to hand any more over to be treated in the same manner so the official response was "Sorry. No! They are all spoken for" which was partially true.

The next incident was bizarre as two boys called out from deep within the recesses "Sir! There's a girl in our shower!" … and there was. The communal shower area had a door into each changing room, one of which contained a couple of teenage females who felt they must take a peep. Les Frogs femmes fatales!

Now to the official reception at the enormous Gothic town hall. I was at great pains to ascertain if it was suitable for pre-teenage boys but was smilingly assured that it was. This was either a huge pork pie (lie) or a terrible mistake. Read on ……..

The reception was lavish – too lavish as it turned out. The array of champagne was quite the biggest I have ever seen so I immediately told my team that under no circumstances were they to partake of any alcohol and that soft drinks were the order of the day. Absolutely no champagne! If you have, or have had, or have ever known a 12 year old boy, however, then you will know that whatever you forbid, he is tempted to do the opposite. In any case I had been told the speeches would be short. Regrettably, they weren't and I found myself trapped at the front of the official gathering. I just hoped my team were behaving themselves.

The first sign of trouble came when my assistant muscled his way through to the front of the reception during the mayor's speech and whispered "Come quick. There's trouble downstairs." "Is it urgent?" I heard myself say but when I received the response "Yes. The boys are playing dodgems and deliberately running in front of moving trams in the town square" I knew it was.

I guessed what had happened – although I had no idea just how much of it had happened – and glowered at the beautiful French waitresses as I sped past them. I just knew they had taken pity on my little cherubs and encouraged them to partake of the generous French hospitality behind my back. "Oh, mes cheries, just a leetle will not harm you!" Oh, les Frogs femmes fatales!

The situation in the square was dire but by the time I arrived the urchins, pre-warned, had fled but it did not take a genius to work out where they had gone to ground. A games machine shop round the corner proved a magnet for the by now inebriated little monsters so in I marched ready for battle. A loud cry of "Out!" was enough for all but two to scuttle through the exit as fast as their little legs would carry them, giving me a very wide berth on the way. Sir was not happy and they knew it. The remaining two brazen individuals, however, said "Won't be a minute, sir!" as they carried on playing with their one-armed bandits. This was too much! In a single movement I scooped one up under my right arm and the other under my left, then bodily carried them out into the street as an astonished adult clientele stared in blank amazement at two small English schoolchildren disappearing horizontally head first at speed through the door.

Back at the hostel all evening leave was cancelled, apart from one of a pair of twins who had obeyed my alcohol ban. By now very subdued the team was waiting for the Sword of Damocles to fall. It did but not in the way they expected. Inspector Clouseau quickly discovered his initial theory was correct. The young French waitresses had egged on my "Angels Anglaises" during the boring official speeches and my little cupids had been only too willing to try the proffered drinks. One glassful might just have done no harm but two boys admitted to drinking eight … I repeat … eight glasses of champagne! My solution was swift and sure "You will each spend 30 seconds under a freezing cold shower for every glass you drank!" It had a sobering effect, both literally and metaphorically. I made the biggest culprits wait till last and made sure the earlier frozen customers heard their pleading squeals to be let out. Oh no you don't! They served their full term and emerged a gentle shade of light blue. Serves 'em right.

I would like to say both these characters behaved perfectly for the rest of the trip. They did for me but one of them cheeked an older boy on the way home at a motorway service station and ended up in a prickly bush for his trouble. When his parents enquired as to how exactly he had managed to get so scratched during a rugby match I took great pleasure in telling them the truth. On hearing the saga of the champagne flutes his father said "Serves 'im right" I rest my case m'lud.

The following are extracts from notes I made during the trip:

Teacher 1 – "It's 60% proof so don't let Janice light a fag near it."

Teacher 2 – Looking at a large ornamental fountain in the town square: "That's a jolly big bidet over there."

Teacher 3 – "Michael Richards is buying something." Teacher 4 – "Probably a brain. He couldn't get one on the NHS."

Teacher 4 again – "I've got my two salami rolls, now you can give the rest to the boys." Two minutes later – "I've got all the kiwi fruits, you can give the apples and bananas to the boys."

Teacher 1 – "I'll pay you not to write that down." Me – "How much?"

Teacher 2 after a meal out – "Has anyone got any money to pay the bill?"

Teacher 3 – "It would be anti-social to leave those two cognacs on the table."

Teacher 4 on being handed a large French roll – "You only need one of these to last the whole day." Teacher 2 – "Would you like another one?" Teacher 4 - "Yes please."

Teacher 1 – "Is that a hosepipe James Smith is using behind that bus?" It wasn't, as evidenced when the bus suddenly moved off and James and four others hastily turned their hosepipes in the opposite direction. Well it had been a long journey and there were no toilets at this stop off point! Fortunately, it was an all male trip – apart from Janice, the lady teacher!

Teacher 2 – "Never mind what might happen in France. That boy would get lost between his desk and the waste paper bin while sharpening his pencil."

The prize for the most insensitive remark of the whole trip, however, went to Teacher 4 who said to the French organiser: "Is the lady cooking breakfast the Roman Catholic priest's housekeeper?" "No." "Oh, is she his wife then? Whoops, sorry!"

It was run pretty close, though, by a brief dispute on the coach home when a 14 year old boy challenged me over something to which I replied: "Are you calling me a liar?" "Yes!" was his reply, at which point all the other teachers slid quietly down into their seats awaiting the inevitable explosion. It came – after which they slowly emerged to see the boy, having realised his massive mistake, make a grovelling apology.

The coach arrived at Calais ready to board the ferry but two teachers were bursting for the loo so got off to find the nearest gents, promising to be back a.s.a.p. No sooner had they disappeared round the corner, however, then the coach was beckoned forward on to the ferry so when the duo returned it had gone. Panic stations as, not knowing which ferry we were booked on they tried to bluff their way aboard the wrong ship. I was unaware of these shenanigans but decided it was not my problem and settled down on one of the few remaining seats on

Pride of Bruges. Departure time came and went, then the loudspeaker boomed: "This is your captain speaking. Sorry about the delay but we had to wait for two latecomers." The lady next to me turned and said "Some people can't be trusted. Probably teachers." I heartily agreed then suffered acute embarrassment as the two culprits, all hot and bothered, came up to me and apologised for keeping the ship waiting. The lady next to me turned away. I wonder why?

The saga was not over yet because when the alarm sounded in one of the onboard shops I was hastily informed everything was in hand by the head of sixth form. I later discovered one of his charges had nicked a bottle of brandy but that was nothing to how I was kept in conversation by another colleague while, I later discovered, his chums were loading several crates of beer into the other side of the coach which they had just bought at a French hypermarket.

It was two teachers missing when we boarded but it was three boys missing when we docked. A search party found someone being seasick in the toilets but, in between gurgles, he flatly refused to identify himself. "He can't be one of ours" said Teacher number 1 " … his feet are too big!" Wrong because it transpired he was one of our missing trio. The other two were eventually located wandering round the wrong car deck after the coach had gone ashore.

The best is left till last. Teacher number 1 on BBC Local Radio a couple of days later said: "I'm head of languages at St. Chad's School and we enjoyed the French exchange a very lot." He is now headmaster of a large comprehensive school?

PS When we were asked to return the favour of a French exchange to England and we tried to find some host families, one pupil came out with "My dad said 'If I needed a frog I could go to the local pond and catch one'" Hmmmm!

GREAT UNCLE BULGARIA

If you have never seen *The Wombles* then this story might be wasted on you!

It was assembly time but it was also April Fools Day and I was quite sure something silly would be attempted. Being a Northerner who called a spade a spade rather than a trenching instrument, I was prepared for anything and could share a joke with the best of them but, alas, this was a staid grammar school with little sense of humour and hardly any teaching staff under the age of 40.

The initial prayers went well but when the music teacher plunged his hands down on to the organ nothing happened.

There was to be no *Bread of Heaven* today and it later transpired the fuse had been removed. Undaunted he switched to the grand piano but several well placed hymn books on the strings inside meant he sounded more like Winifred Atwell performing *Plink, Plank, Plunk*. As the former organist at a well known cathedral he was not terribly amused. His dignity had been dented but he tried to stay calm although undoubtedly inwardly seething. Assembly was his big moment of the week.

Cutting his losses the headmaster abandoned the hymn and announced *The Lord's Prayer*. Just as it began, however, from behind the stage curtains at full volume suddenly boomed "Underground, overground, wombling free, the Wombles of Wimbledon Common are we". It was the well-known *Wombles Song* which was all the rage at the time. The tuneful sound of Bernard Cribbins, however, was not quite what was anticipated at morning assembly but the pupils were highly amused and I swear some of them joined in before the deputy head disappeared behind the curtains, and removed the needle from the cunningly concealed record player.

The headmaster and all the older staff were outraged. "The

culprit will report to my office immediately after assembly" boomed the boss while I inwardly but secretly chuckled to myself. Who dunnit? I soon found out.

I was very much the youngest of four housemasters and it turned out to be one of my prefects who was coming on camp as a junior leader that summer. He had been dared by various others but had not expected quite such a backlash. The song was supposed to have come on instead of the hymn but misfortune dictated otherwise and the slight delay meant it came on in competition with "Our Father, Who art in Heaven …."

I suspect "Our Father" was probably as amused as I was because there is nothing worse than a pontificating Pharisee. All Christians and churchgoers need to be able to laugh at themselves but – if you will pardon the metaphor - the music had to be faced. As feared, he was demoted from his role as school prefect and an official notice went up to that effect, signed "G. Howarth – Headmaster".

My house assembly took place the following morning and I, quite daringly, announced at the end that, despite his misdemeanours in assembly the previous day, James Horn would remain a house prefect. There was a spontaneous burst of applause which I had not expected and, sensing the delicacy of the situation, not one of them ever leaked my comments back to senior staff.

As I departed for my first lesson I noticed that something new had been added to the official notice because underneath the word "Headmaster", it read simply, "Great Uncle Bulgaria"! I quietly chuckled and kept mum.

UP AND DOWN
THE MONUMENT

If you want a child to disobey you then the best way is to forbid them from doing something. Taking 200 pupils to London was always a risky business but the advantages usually outweighed the disadvantages. For many it was their first, and possibly last visit to the Metropolis and almost certainly their first trip on the Underground, not to mention exploring many famous places they would only otherwise see on TV.

London Zoo, *HMS Belfast*, London Transport Museum, Tower of London, St. Paul's, the River Thames, Westminster Abbey – the list is endless but one star attraction was The Monument. On the site of Pudding Lane by the former Billingsgate Fish Market, Wren's majestic impressive circular column stands aloof. Sadly, it is now surrounded by modern office blocks but this was not the case more than 30 years ago when I took my first group there.

Our numbers were too great to go up all at once so I staggered them but always ensured a teacher remained at the top. As each group went up in turn I made a point of saying "Be careful and make sure nothing is thrown from the top." Some hopes!

I remained in charge at the bottom and hoped everyone would heed instructions but when I spotted a couple of *HMS Belfast* tickets come fluttering down, I knew they hadn't. This was not inherently dangerous in itself but it was bad form and also disobedience. I was rather disappointed and felt let down but I knew which class was up there and I was jolly well going to find out who the culprit was. Rather than challenge them when they came down, however, I decided to use it as an illustration when I saw them for R.E. the following day.

Having explained the danger of throwing things off high buildings and my disappointment at someone being disobedient I called their bluff. The secret of psychological warfare is to convince the enemy you know more than he does so towards the end of the lesson I said "I know exactly who it was and I expect you to own up, apologise and accept your punishment at my study immediately after the lesson".

The word "you" can be both single and plural and in this case I honestly meant it as singular. Much to my astonishment, however, it turned out to be plural. Having put everything away I retreated to my room hoping that someone had a conscience. "You" turned out to be eight consciences all lined up in a neat row awaiting the Sword of Damocles. I was impressed in a paradoxical sort of way.

Each was offered an after school detention or one stroke of the slipper. Each readily took the latter and disappeared through the door rather more quickly than they had entered. Strangely (or perhaps not) my future relationship with this class

was enhanced by this episode but only those over the age of about 50 could possibly understand why. "Esprit de corps" does not come lightly and if you still don't understand what it means then I suggest you watch the 1955 film *Cockleshell Heroes* where a rag bag of volunteers are transformed by rigorous discipline into an elite corps of Marine commandos, all but two of whom perish in an act of derring-do.

Three other illustrations spring to mind. One former pupil had a great sense of humour and when his own son (now a GP) was old enough to attend one of my camps he greeted me on his arrival with "I've got a surprise for you!" With that he shouted "Horace!" at which an ancient arthritic dog crawled slowly from the back of his car and obediently limped towards us. "I named him after your pet slipper, sir. Remember when you used him on me?" Well I didn't as it happened but he assured me he fully deserved it and that it had a beneficial effect. It must have done because he later played cricket for England after which, at my suggestion, he became a successful housemaster at a famous public school.

Another pupil with a fine sense of humour and a cheeky grin to match is now, like his father and grandfather before him, a famous racing jockey. I once took him for maths in a classroom some distance from my own so I was invariably late. On this occasion, however, I turned up on time but on entering the building was surprised to hear a passable imitation of my own accent emanating from within so, silently, I approached the classroom and peeped round the door. I was spotted by the class but not by the joker who had his back to me, so I put my finger to my lips and we all enjoyed listening to his mockery for another couple of minutes. Only when he paused did I applaud and sit at his desk telling him to continue with the lesson as he was doing so well. If you can imagine a bright shade of beetroot then you can imagine the colour of his face, the same shade as a student at university who once unwittingly mimicked his Professor of Theology who always prayed before each lecture. Thinking he had not yet arrived the student intoned in a very high voice: "Let us pray" only to receive an echo from behind the door in an equally high pitched tone: "We already have done. Please sit down!"

The third incident came to my attention after I received an amusing e-mail from the wife of a church pastor from inner Liverpool which said "What a pity you weren't in church on Sunday morning because my husband had the whole place in hysterics explaining how you gave him the slipper for being cheeky! He based the whole sermon on authority and personal discipline." A couple of years earlier my daughter had rung me from university all excited with "Dad, you're never going to believe this but …." She then went on to explain how she had gone to a student dinner where the guest speaker was a local pastor who talked about the influence of his former football teacher. No name was mentioned but she listened intently and at the end went up to him and said "I think you've been talking about my dad!" He had and it led to a joyful reunion soon afterwards.

Believe me when I say there is nothing more rewarding than being thanked years later by a former pupil and I hope that warm glow was experienced by my former art teacher whom I looked up annually after he moved to Devon. He stood by me when things were difficult at home and I never forgot his quiet concern. He also told me several funny anecdotes about other school teachers but that, as they say, is another story. He made sure I was also impaled on a school slipper on more than one occasion and he was absolutely right to do so. I owed it to my own pupils to repeat his care and concern. I hope, and believe that I did although you can't win them all and not every one was successful ……

FAILURES

No teacher ever achieves 100% success with his pupils. It just doesn't happen because social chemistry precludes it. Given a supportive parent, however, then the chances of success, although not guaranteed, improve enormously.

My rapport with a certain class was excellent and each morning they were as pleased to see me as I was to see them. One day, however, two of them cheated in a maths lesson. It was obvious to me, it was obvious to them and it was obvious to the rest of the class – so I wrote "You are a cheat!" on the relevant page of their exercise book. One of them went as bright as a beetroot while the other said "Sorry, sir!"

I thought no more about it until the headmaster summoned me towards the end of the week and said one of the parents had

complained. I immediately knew which one because the other boy (the beetroot) was the second son of a colleague and pleaded with me afterwards "Please don't tell my dad, sir. He'll kill me!" The headmaster tore out the offending page and I thought to myself how that particular pupil might easily come a cropper in the future. Alternatively, he could be a millionaire by now. The beetroot, I am pleased to say, went on to qualify as a doctor. Splendid!

Taking a pupil who has been expelled from another school is always difficult and in one case I ended up with an overnight swastika painted on my front door at home. I got off lightly compared to my neighbours in the road, however, one of whom had his car set alight by the same idiot. Incredibly, the father denied his son was responsible but the early morning milkman had seen him in the act and a successful prosecution followed.

During my teaching career I lost on average about one former pupil a year, the majority from wholly avoidable road accidents – some on motorbikes, some on four wheels. At least four others met untimely ends by other means which I will not describe here but the worst incident of all involved four boys in the same car, each of whom I had either warned or disciplined at some time previously. The car hit a lamp post at high speed in the small hours with the occupants under the influence of several stimulants.

The youngest passenger was the saddest. Soon after being expelled from his previous school his poor behaviour resurrected itself. Eventually I had had enough and, finding him outside the music room from which he had been ejected for the umpteenth time, I decided to tell him his pedigree. Pinning him up against the wall I told him in no uncertain manner that unless he changed his ways then he would be dead within six months. I was wrong – he was dead within six weeks. How sad is that?

I was threatened by several drunken parents and I was even assaulted outside my own home by a former pupil who had been expelled. It was a good job the other deputy head was with me at the time. On another occasion a young man burst into my office at 8am and demanded to know if I was a teacher. "I am the deputy headmaster." "You'll do!" He then went into a tirade, quite what about I am still not sure but he did not look old enough to be the father of the small boy cowering behind him, a new pupil I had yet to meet. It transpired he was a 21 year old stepfather but I was no wiser at what had lit his blue touch paper by the time he stormed off.

On another occasion, having given up my Saturday afternoon to run a district football trial, I was pleased when a parent came into the staff changing room and thanked me and my two colleagues for being so generous with our time. No sooner had he left, however, than a small clearly drunken specimen barged in and started effing and blinding. Having told me I knew nothing about football (I am a qualified F.A. Coach with a great deal of experience right up to county level) and having threatened to put my "effing head through the effing wall", he stormed out again. When we recovered our composure we ventured out to try and find who he was and, more importantly, who his son was.

The latter turned out to be a new arrival at my own school who, given his home circumstances, turned out remarkably well. Having established the man's identity I rang the local police who laughed and said they knew all about him. He was estranged from his wife but regularly ill-treated her. Would I like them to pay him a visit? Yes I would because that could solve everything – and it did. His son later played for the school and district teams and father occasionally turned up as a silent and well-behaved spectator. I don't think the word "apology" was in his vocabulary though, especially as, by his own admission, he had failed to make it as a professional footballer – hence his pent up frustration.

Beware a drunken Irishman! I unexpectedly met one as I was telling off a boy in the corridor outside a science room. In through the open door from the playground staggered a man I had not met before but I knew exactly who he was and how to handle him. When he came menacingly towards me and said something like "Shleeve thar boy alone!" I pushed the pupil back into the lab (much to the teacher's surprise because she had only just ejected him) and headed for the school office where I rang the police. The gentleman in question was a dangerous animal as my next door neighbour, a female probation officer, had already told me he had threatened her with his shotgun which he (presumably illegally) kept on a chair at home.

When a massive West Indian with a Rastafarian hat walked into the playground and literally thrust his head through the headmaster's open window and demanded to know "Where's Winston?" we hastily replied "He's not here today". After the intruder departed I quickly sought out the equally large pupil and warned him he was on the menu of someone even bigger than him. Their potential confrontation was either drug- or girl friend-related and I wanted it to occur well away from school.

A rather sadder unexpected visitor was a young man who somehow managed to find his way into the internal quadrangle where he started running around in circles past several classroom windows. This caused great excitement among the pupils until I intervened and brought his mini-Olympics to an abrupt halt. Quickly realising he was sixpence short of a shilling I called the police who came and collected this sadly damaged member of society and returned him to the nearby hospital.

I did have one successful confrontation though. Hearing that a former pupil was in school brandishing a plank with a large protruding nail, I decided to try and stop him. We met in the corridor, he looking for revenge on a fifth former (Year 11) who he thought had pinched his girl friend, and me barring his way. It was a bit like the stand off near the end of *Gunfight at the OK Corral*. I heard myself say "Put it down and come to my office so we can talk about it." He muttered something about getting out of his way and knocking seven bells out of his enemy but I stood my ground and repeated myself several times. After what seemed like an eternity he relaxed his previously tense muscles, dropped the plank by his side and meekly followed me to my study where we talked out his problems.

Before he left school the previous term I had challenged him about glue sniffing but, true to form, any drug addict always comes up with a convincing story. He now poured his heart out and said how grateful he was for me stopping him doing something silly and also remembered with gratitude how I had dealt sensitively with an unfortunate medical accident some years earlier. It was all quite humbling. He shook my hand before departing – sans plank with nail – while I reflected on another job well done. Was this why I came into the teaching profession?

My reward? I was made redundant the following year but – as it turned out – it was a blessing in disguise and I eventually launched out into a totally different but equally fulfilling career. How I wish I could say the same about my 11 loyal colleagues who lost their jobs at the same time as me – plus all those ousted in the ensuing years. Life is not fair and trying to teach in a sink school is probably the most unfair of all. You are damned if you succeed and damned if you don't!

Failures? I am not so sure. About ten of my former charges became full time church ministers and pastors, including two influential bishops. You decide!

HOWLERS

All the following are genuine although some came from teachers at other schools. I am not irreverent but, when teaching R.E., I never could resist drawing a picture of an ice cream sundae with a gloomy-looking face on the top every time I saw the following regular mistake in a pupil's exercise book – "Jesus in the dessert."

Try the following true R.E. answers for starters:

1. Jesus preached the Sermon in the Mouth.
2. Which religious group criticised Jesus? The Parasites.
3. At the Last Supper Jesus and his disciples ate roast turkey, chicken legs, potatoes, crusty rolls and a bottle of wine. They all went away happy.
4. Peter had a vision and was visited by one of God's angles.
5. After being baptised Jesus went straight into the dessert.
6. They hurried the burial of Jesus to keep his body fresh.
7. They hurried the burial of Jesus to stop his body going funny.
8. When they met Jesus on the road to Emmaus he had a spear coming out of his side.
9. Joseph and Mary went to Bethlehem to be censured.
10. Jesus was born in Bethlehem because he was under two years old.
11. Parable of the Lost Sheep in your own words – "The shepherd left the 99 sheep having a party and went out with his blow torch to find the missing one. It took him ages though and by the time he found it he was tired so rode it back home."

Now try these for your main course:

12. In the first book of the Bible, Guinness, God got tired of creating the world so he took the Sabbath off.

13. Adam and Eve were created from an apple tree. Noah built an ark and the animals came on in pears. Noah's wife was Joan of Ark.

14. Lot's wife was a pillar of salt during the day but a ball of fire during the night.

15. The Jews were a proud people and throughout history they had trouble with unsympathetic Genitals.

16. Samson was a strongman who let himself be led astray by a Jezebel like Delilah.

17. Samson slayed the Philistines with the axe of the apostles.

18. Moses led the Jews to the Red Sea where they made unleavened bread which is bread without any ingredients.

19. The Egyptians were all drowned in the dessert. Afterwards, Moses went up to Mount Cyanide to get the Ten Commandments

20. The first commandment was when Eve told Adam to eat the apple.

21. The seventh commandment is "Thou shalt not admit adultery".

22. The greatest miracle in the Bible was when Joshua told his son to stand still and he obeyed him.

23. David was a Hebrew king who was skilled at playing the liar. He fought the Finkelsteins, a race of people who lived in Biblical times.

24. Solomon, one of David's sons, had 300 wives and 700 porcupines.

25. When Mary heard she was the mother of Jesus, she sang the Magna Carta.

26. When the three wise guys from the east side arrived they found Jesus in the manager.

27. Jesus was born because Mary had an immaculate contraption.

28. St. John the blacksmith dumped water on his head.

29. Jesus enunciated the golden rule, which says to do unto others before they do one to you. He also explained a man doth not live by sweat alone.

23. It was a miracle when Jesus rose from the dead and managed to get the tombstone off the entrance.

31. The people who followed the Lord were called the 12 Decibels.

32. The Epistles were the wives of the Apostles.

33. One of the opossums was St. Matthew who was also a taximan.

34. St. Paul cavorted to Christianity and preached holy acrimony which is another name for marriage.

35. Christians have only one spouse. This is called monotony.

Now for the dessert:

36. Ancient Egypt was old. It was inhabited by gypsies and mummies who all wrote in hydraulics. They lived in the Sarah Dessert whose climate is such that all the inhabitants have to live somewhere else.

37. The Greeks were a highly sculptured people and without them we wouldn't have history. The Greeks also had myths. A myth is a young female moth.

38. Socrates was a famous old Greek teacher who went around giving people advice. They killed him. He later died from an overdose of wedlock which is apparently poisonous. After his death, his career suffered a dramatic decline.

39. In the first Olympic games, Greeks ran races, jumped, hurled biscuits, and threw the java. The games were messier than they show on TV now.

40. Julius Caesar extinguished himself on the battlefields of Gaul. The Ides of March murdered him because they thought he was going to be made king. Dying, he gasped out "Same to you, Brutus."

41. Joan of Arc was burnt to a steak and was canonized by Bernard Shaw for reasons I don't really understand. The English and French still have problems.

42. Queen Elizabeth was the "Virgin Queen." As a queen she was a success. When she exposed herself before her troops they all shouted "Hurrah!" and that was the end of the fighting for a long while.

43. Sir Francis Drake circumcised the world with a 100 foot clipper which was very dangerous for all his men.

44. The greatest writer of the Renaissance was William Shakespeare. He was born in the year 1564, supposedly on his birthday. He never made much money and is famous only because of his plays. He wrote tragedies, comedies, and hysterectomies, all in Islamic pentameter.

45. Johann Bach wrote a great many musical compositions and had a large number of children. In between he practiced on an old spinster which he kept in the attic. Bach died from 1750 to the present. He was the most famous composer in the world and so was Handel. Handel was half German, half Italian, and half English.

46. Beethoven wrote music even though he was deaf. He was so deaf that he wrote loud music and became the father of rock and roll. He took long walks in the forest even when everyone was calling for him. Beethoven expired in 1827 and later died for this.

47. Louis Pasteur discovered a cure for rabbits but I don't know why.

48. Madman Curie discovered radio. She was the first woman to do what she did. Other women have become scientists since her but they didn't get to find radios because they were already taken.

49. Benjamin Franklin discovered electricity by rubbing two cats backward and also declared, "A horse divided against itself cannot stand." He was a naturalist for sure. Franklin died in 1790 and is still dead.

50. Q: Who invented the aqualung? A: Lady Godiva!

And to finish off with? The best of the lot:

51. Charles Darwin was a naturist. He wrote the Organ of the Species. It was very long so people got upset about it and had trials to see if it was really true. I don't get it.

FORTY YEARS ON ...

Keeping in touch with ex-pupils has its rewards and I was absolutely delighted when a former junior football captain contacted me to say he wanted to organise a team reunion 40 years after we scored 100 goals before Christmas, the bribe for which I used at the time was a picture in the local paper. It worked but it was a close run thing because with only five minutes to go in the final match there were still only 99 goals on the board. There were no histrionics, however, when the centre forward hammered in the centennial goal, merely a "Well done" from me on the sidelines and a few handshakes on the pitch. Everyone was glowing afterwards, though, and "Please sir. have we earned the picture?" was answered in the affirmative.

144

The captain's plan was to track down every player and put them into another photo – this time in colour – replicating the exact positions of the earlier one. I couldn't wait to see what they all looked like but first we had to track them down. The captain was brilliant and tried every trick he knew but, with less than a fortnight to go, he still had one to find. He then located the whereabouts of his sister and she pointed us in the direction of Cornwall. Could he come up to London for the reunion? He could, and he did.

The day dawned and I chuckled when I saw several of them were now balder than me and it was just like old times as I refereed an impromptu kick about in the new sports hall just like I had done in the old gym. Equally pleasing, it finished as an honourable score draw, after which it was time for a reunion tea followed by a speech from me.

I regaled them with several school stories about teachers they remembered and I saw no harm in divulging a few trade secrets. One such classic was a naïve young teacher who borrowed, without permission which would never, ever have been given, the immaculate plimsolls of the head of P.E. who was a Services man and a stickler for discipline. I was minding my own business in the staffroom when a clap of thunder came charging through the door. With a murderous shout of "Your feet in my shoes! How dare you! How old are you? Why did you take them?" he lambasted the stupid clot who compounded the situation by saying "My own shoes were dirty!" At this there was another volcanic explosion before the older man tore the shoes from the feet of the hapless youngster who had covered them in mud on a cross country run. You just couldn't make it up. Even I was quaking as the thunder clap vanished and the door nearly fell off its hinges as it slammed shut. It was some time before the shaking white-faced cross country runner even dared to move!

Another new teacher had never played cricket but thought he would like to try (sounds like something from Gilbert and Sullivan's *The Mikado*), so was picked for the next staff match. It was carefully explained to him how, why and where he needed to place his "box" (a circular item of plastic equipment to protect the vital masculine parts) but nobody told him he should wear it inside his trousers! I must say the sight of a batsman wobbling ungainly to the crease with a box strapped to the outside of his cricket whites reminded me of Donald Duck. Shades of Brian Johnston's gaffe when, after a batsman was doubled up in agony after being hit in the aforesaid area, he managed to take guard again only for the commentator to unwittingly say "Here comes the bowler. One ball left!" Another unforgettable gaffe was "The bowler's Holding, the batsman's Willey!" while a Spoonerism should have come out as "The umpire's sitting on a shooting stick" – but it didn't! True!

Having been put right on his batting, our rookie teacher later tried his hand at bowling but when the batsman gave his first delivery an almighty wallop it flew straight back at him at high speed. In a frantic attempt to get out of the way, however, he succeeded in trapping the ball straight up his armpit. As he naively retrieved it everyone else shouted "Howzat!?" The bowler and the batsman looked at each other equally non-plussed and as the umpire raised his finger the latter seemed decidedly reluctant to trudge back to the pavilion. Who could blame him?

Everyone agreed we did daft things when we were young and I must have been mad to pack 11 boys in a Morris Minor and 17 in a Ford Anglia estate. Amazingly, there were no safety rules in those days and I also took delight in supervising as many boys as we could pack into a phone box during one Easter holiday on the Isle of Wight. I can't remember how many we managed to squash in but I do remember another boy rushing up to join in the fun only to trip and smash his face against the kiosk, neatly snapping both his top front teeth in two. His father was not terribly amused when we returned home.

Then I was asked about the infamous five ball over in a staff match. Had it really happened? Yes it had. The umpire – a qualified MCC umpire no less – made sure we all knew about his reputation but had it shattered in several tiny pieces by the very first ball of the game. In what was obviously a well-rehearsed ploy the school fast bowler ran up and pretended to deliver the ball while the wicketkeeper and all five of the slips leapt up in unison and shouted "Howzat!?" Incredibly, the umpire put his finger up and said to me (I was the batsman at the non-striker's end), "That was so quick I never even saw it!" I shared what I thought was his joke, the batsman stood his ground and the over began again. It was only when the umpire called "Over" after just five balls that I realised he thought the non-delivery had actually taken place. Later in the same match, I had the satisfaction of bowling the school's star player, a future county captain and England international. Truth to tell he took an almighty heave at what I intended as an outswinger only for it to inexplicably move the other way and remove his middle stump. Ah – memories!

I finished my speech by showing I had also been a bit of a lad too in my youth. As a 21-year-old tent leader on a camp one summer I willingly assisted some slightly older staff officers on a night time raid on another camp down the coast. We had already demolished various items of equipment when there was a gurgling sound followed by the strangled voice of the activities officer saying "Oh no. I've knocked one of the elsans over!" An elsan is a portable toilet by the way and as there was no way we could clean up the mess in the dark we scarpered as fast as we could. You will not be surprised to hear their camp leader complained to ours and the five of us were paraded in front of him like naughty schoolboys. The fact that the one who organised the raid was already a teacher made no difference. The leader was very large, very Scottish and very cross. After telling us our pedigree he said "I'm so angry, I'm going to report you all to the Camps Secretary in London" to which the activities officer replied "Go ahead. I am the Camps Secretary in London!" Game, set and match!

A DAY IN THE LIFE OF A DEPUTY HEADMASTER

Believe it or not, my diary tells me all these events happened on the same day but you probably won't believe it.

Arriving early I receive five phone calls telling me five teachers are away ill. A great start but at least they know they have to ring before 8am. Now …. unless I can persuade five supply teachers to come in and cover, then at least two of their classes will end up on extended litter duty which for many will be a welcome relief from academic rigour. Did I say rigour? Well academic anyway …. I think.

Phone call number six is from a member of the public who informs me a second year pupil has been blown off his bike into a car and, following a 999 call from a passer by, has been taken to hospital with a suspected broken ankle.

Ian, aged 14, comes into my office because he wants to talk confidentially to me about his family violence the previous night.

Good year 9 Music lesson about Bix Beiderbecke, Louis Armstrong and the history of recorded jazz.

Lee, aged 13, is absent from Maths and has apparently run home. A quick investigation reveals he has assaulted three other boys. Having told his mother he has been assaulted himself she turns up at school ready for action with the proverbial rolling pin.

Brett, also aged 13, is absent from Geography and has also run home with a cock and bull story. Father arrives to be told his son has been reprimanded for throwing litter in the corridor. Father doesn't believe it so Brett later throws food around in

the dining hall for good measure.

Ben, age 15, throws a chair across the room during a drama lesson – how appropriate – and later storms out of afternoon registration. Ten minutes later he takes part in a buffalo run down the main corridor which comes to an abrupt halt when my fellow deputy head appears at the far end of the thoroughfare. The buffaloes hastily abort their stampede, turn sharp left and leg it out on to the playground.

Good Year 8 Geography class explaining how the Egyptians use the Archimedean Screw to irrigate their fields.

In a hurry to unlock my door I jam the key in upside down!

Jane aged 13 wants to know if we get an extra hour off school when the clocks go back next week!

Winston turns up with what can only be described as an unusually flat hairstyle. Apparently it is called an "aircraft carrier" and when the headmaster asks how much it cost, the answer takes away the breath of all three senior teachers who unwittingly chorus in unison: "How much?"

Jimmy saunters in 25 minutes late so I tell him to report to his teacher at once – which turns out to be me.

The headmaster asks if I will take over tomorrow's 4C visit to Clearwell Caves because the remedial teacher lost control of 3C there yesterday who promptly released a flock of sheep from a paddock which jumped the queue and joined the other tourists inside the caves!

Mark, aged 15 and none too bright, thinks it a good idea to unplug the fire hose in the changing rooms. Having turned it on he cannot find the stopcock to turn it off and by the time I arrive the gym is under water. A game of basketball turns into a game of water polo and a new set of dry shirts is required for the Under 14 football match after school.

A quick visit to the feeder primary school down the road turns into a nightmare as I unknowingly walk into the wrong end and wait until the head teacher finishes shouting at some children for fighting, Only then do I discover I am in the infants department. A quick detour to the door at the other end of the playground finds me waiting while the other head teacher shouts at some pupils for fighting. No wonder we have so much trouble.

Irritated by girls talking behind his back while writing on the board, the French teacher turns round sharply and accidentally decapitates the daffodils on his window sill with a metre rule – or should that be a yardstick?

After being told off for being rude to a dinner supervisor, Jason legs it home and mother arrives to complain complete with her hair in curlers.

The English teacher brings two boys to me for letting off a stink bomb. I agree not to punish them if they will go back to the joke shop and let off another one there to see how the owner likes it! He didn't!

Liam and Grant are brought to me after being caught fighting in the playground.

Good Year 7 History lesson on the Romans.

Mustafa and Hakim are caught running round the corridors when they should have been in History where the teacher has failed to spot their absence. As I deliver them I discover a scene of mayhem caused by a wallet going missing with £40 in it. What, you may ask, is a 12 year old boy doing at school with £40 in cash? Don't ask! Just as I am about to adopt a cross between Sherlock Holmes, Darth Vader and Action Man, I am informed that Mrs. Jones has arrived with her son, David, who has mysteriously run home with a wallet containing £40 in cash which he said he "found" on the way to school. Hmmm.

Melanie aged 12 wants me to investigate a rash on her body so I gently point her in the direction of a senior female colleague.

Her brother James, aged 14, then turns up with a similar complaint which I quickly identify as German Measles. Off home my lad – and probably your sister too.

My younger son rings to tell me he has lost the key to his padlock and can't unlock his bike. I tell him to walk home from school which I hope will teach him a lesson until I later discover he had borrowed my bike!

Only six out of 12 members of 5C turn up for my Maths test, four of whom have no pen or pencil.

Geoffrey nips in the ladies toilet and steals a teacher's handbag!

The day is over and it's time for my after-school football club in the gym. Nothing can go wrong here … can it? Yes it can as a triangular fight breaks out in the changing room resulting in one boy running away and head butting the gym door which has just been closed in his face as he was looking the other way. Before I can intervene, his pursuer aims a wild kick, misses and jams his toe under the door! I greet his screams of supposed agony with "If you don't shut up, I won't let you take part tonight." An immediate outbreak of peace occurs as the owner of the supposedly injured toe says "Oh. OK then!" His injured digit is carefully extracted and checked for damage which turns out to be superficial. The other two sides of the fight commiserate with him and all three end up shaking hands.

The evening is a success, ending as usual with a vigorous bout of British Bulldog, complete with bangs and bruises soothed by happy singing and splashing in the shower afterwards.

*A lone dad turns up to take his offspring home and I casually remark that it's time for bed. His reply takes me aback, however; "Oh no. I've hired an X-rated video we're going to watch." No wonder he was late for school the following morning.

I stagger home, fall into bed and dream of more excitement at the fun factory tomorrow.

*This lead me to investigate television and video habits amongst the pupils, the results of which were so appalling the headmaster decided to make them public. They caused an initial outcry and even appeared as a question on Radio 4's *The News Quiz* but more than 30 years later nobody disagrees any more – except programme makers and producers intent on making money at the expense of others. Worst of all, during the years in between we have lost our sense of shock and have become thoroughly desensitised to gratuitous violence and pornography.

YOU COULDN'T
MAKE IT UP

As a deputy headmaster I kept a diary of events which one day I vowed to publish. Some of the incidents are so bizarre you really couldn't make them up but here are just a few to tickle the pallet. Many others are unprintable.

****

Intercepting a girl walking down the corridor in the middle of a lesson I asked: "Where are you going?" She replied: "To see Miss Rogers." "We haven't got a Miss Rogers!" It turned out to be Mr. Hodges!

****

A workman accidentally locked the keys in his car so asked to borrow a hammer from the CDT Department to smash a side window. A 14 year old boy overheard him and said "Don't do that. I'll break in for you!" ... and he did!

****

Overheard in a drama lesson: "I wasn't talking. I was only telling her something."

****

As a joke the senior teacher told a boy to stand on his head which he proceeded to do on a chair – just as a joke – but then fell off and landed full on his napper.

****

Letting off a fire alarm was a favourite pastime for some bears of little brain but one managed to cut his hand in the act and was duly arrested as he turned up 30 seconds later for medical treatment in the school office.

****

Note from mother: "Anthony played truant yesterday so I'm not going to let him have this afternoon off to buy a new pair of shoes."

****

When a 15 year old boy turned up soaking wet it turned out he had been thrown in the reservoir on his birthday by his best friend. Before I could say anything he came out with: "It's fair, sir. I threw him in last week!"

****

In a frivolous mood to a class taking notes in a history lesson I said of the Battle of Hastings: "The Normans ran up to the Saxons and said "Yah boo. Can't catch me before running back down the slope." A moment later, pen at the ready, a girl's hand went up and its owner asked "Can you please repeat what they said sir?"

****

Complaint from the local dentist's surgery: "Three of your boys have just run in, shouted 'Fire!' and set the burglar alarm off!" In hot pursuit of the three culprits I passed a noisy class so put my head round the door and said, menacingly: "You're making a racket. Who's supposed to be teaching you?" "You are sir!"

I did the same to another class the following week but this time got a reply from a teacher at the back of the class: "I am!" It was the headmaster.

****

Answer to a question in a science lesson": "A haemophiliac is a woman who can't say 'No' to sex!"

****

When the whole school attended a private showing of the film *Home Alone* I was approached by an irate driver in the cinema car park. "Your pupils refuse to move and I can't get my car out!" It turned out they had been told "Not to move" by my fellow deputy head and were following him to the letter. I negotiated a truce and a way through for the driver, after which the troops immediately closed ranks again – just like the Battle of Waterloo apparently.

****

We were well into St. Paul's Second Missionary Journey in a Year 8 R.E. lesson when Cedric suddenly leapt up with a loud wail and ran to the front shouting "My heart's stopped beating!" I assured him it hadn't and would he please sit down while we continued the lesson. The following week, we were half way through a game of rounders in P.E. when Cedric again suddenly shouted "My heart's stopped beating" but this time legged it in the direction of the changing rooms. This time the class was somewhat less sympathetic and implored me to get on with the game. We did.

****

A note from William Davis's mother: "Please excuse Billy from P.E. coz he's still taking the stair rods." They turned out to be steroids!

****

I raced to an emergency in a CDT lesson where a boy had slipped with a sheet of metal which had cut his wrist through to the bone. After dialling 999 and supervising him being taken away in an ambulance I went back to thank the class for being so helpful and quiet, then turned and opened what I thought was the exit door and walked straight into a cupboard.

★★★★★★★★★★★★★★★★★★★★★★★★

Mark Thompson was late for school. "I had to feed the baby, sir!" A quick phone call to mum resulted in a one word reply: "Rubbish!" It turned out he had been smoking behind the bike sheds.

★★★★★★★★★★★★★★★★★★★★★★★★

Children can be very quick. On spotting a large Canada goose strolling round the quadrangle Jennifer Smith quipped: "It's on an educational visit, sir!"

★★★★★★★★★★★★★★★★★★★★★★★★

My writing was at times not as legible as it might have been – no teacher's scrawl is ever perfect after marking several sets of books but I was finally hoisted with my own petard when a pupil asked: "Please sir, what does this say?" I replied: "You stupid boy! It says 'I can't read your writing!'"

★★★★★★★★★★★★★★★★★★★★★★★★

When a teacher parked the school minibus in a public car park and overstayed his ticket a cunning wheeze was devised whereby an official looking letter on fake headed council notepaper was sent to school demanding a fine of £10. It was signed "A. Pudwin". The teacher fell for it hook, line and sinker and refused to allow the school to pay the fine because it was his fault. Only after he had written out the cheque was it was pointed out that "A. Pudwin" was an anagram of "A Wind up"!

★★★★★★★★★★★★★★★★★★★★★★★★

Mr. Jones rang about a letter telling him his son, Jason, had been playing truant and telling lies – which Jason denied!

★★★★★★★★★★★★★★★★★★★★★★★★

Clint Eastwood (not his real name but we did have a boy named after a famous film star) was sent home with a letter explaining to his father that he had damaged the school wreath on Remembrance Day. His father did not speak English so Clint told him it was about a fictitious school trip to Belgium!

★★★★★★★★★★★★★★★★★★★★★★★★

Many years ago on the Harry Worth Show, he dialled 999 only to get the engaged tone. It was a joke then but not any more. When I was called to the victim of an assault lying on the school playing field, I feared a serious neck injury so dialled 999 and asked for an ambulance. It should have taken seconds rather than minutes as the depot was less than quarter of a mile away so when I heard the siren I thought it was on its way. It wasn't and as the siren faded into the distance I rang again and stressed the urgency of the situation. An unhelpful operator based 30 miles away told me there was no ambulance available. Can you believe it? When I insisted on one I was grudgingly allowed it from a town 10 miles away which finally arrived about 45 minutes after the assault had taken place, the result of what was nicknamed "The Tunnel of Death" where a boy runs the gauntlet through a bunch of punching and kicking "mates". This boy succeeded in getting through relatively unscathed so one unpleasant individual decided to do the job properly. Despite his injuries, however, the victim was too scared to allow a police prosecution.

★★★★★★★★★★★★★★★★★★★★★★★★

A phone call from the school secretary: "Come quick, a boy's shaved his nail off in the sander during a CDT lesson." Superman sprints through the school corridor and arrives in the school office to find a secretary but no boy. "Where is he?" "Lying under the table. He's fainted!"

****

On the way back I come across Charlie from the PE Department doing his fruit with a 13-year-old who had forgotten his games kit – again. Having run out of adjectives to describe the wretched youth Charlie finally shouted "Now go and get changed!" Hmmmm.

****

When I enquired why Charlie Barnett was missing from my bottom set maths lesson one Wednesday afternoon his chums replied: " He's gone to have his photo taken with the rest of his team to prove they didn't cheat on Sunday, sir." When I asked for an explanation I could hardly believe my ears. It seemed the team manager had played two ringers (a euphemism for unregistered players) under false names and after being challenged to prove his team list was accurate, hit on a scheme of getting every alleged player, including the ones who had not played, off school at the same time, driving them to the town 15 miles away and photographing them in their kit on the same pitch. Amazingly, he might have got away with it had I not asked where my missing pupil was because the other four schools involved had all unknowingly released their boys without questioning their forged notes! A hefty fine and suspension was levied on both the team and the manager.

****

There's plenty more and it's all true! You just couldn't make it up!

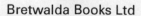

Bretwalda Books Ltd